Quantitatives Controlling

Herausgegeben von
C. Homburg, Köln, Deutschland

Die Schriftenreihe dient als Forum für hervorragende Forschungsergebnisse auf dem Gebiet des Controlling. Ihr liegt ein weites Controllingverständnis zugrunde, das über Problemstellungen der traditionellen internen Unternehmensrechnung hinaus geht und beispielsweise auch Aspekte der Verhaltenssteuerung einschließt.

Der Schwerpunkt der Reihe liegt auf quantitativen Analysen aktueller Controllingfragen. Hierbei werden formal-analytische ebenso wie empirisch ausgerichtete Arbeiten in Betracht gezogen.

Daniel Baumgarten

The Cost Stickiness Phenomenon

Causes, Characteristics, and Implications for Fundamental Analysis and Financial Analysts' Forecasts

Preface by Prof. Dr. Carsten Homburg

Springer Gabler

RESEARCH

Daniel Baumgarten
Cologne, Germany

Dissertation University of Cologne, 2012

ISBN 978-3-8349-4130-5 ISBN 978-3-8349-4131-2 (eBook)
DOI 10.1007/978-3-8349-4131-2

The Deutsche Nationalbibliothek lists this publication in the Deutsche Nationalbibliografie; detailed bibliographic data are available in the Internet at http://dnb.d-nb.de.

Springer Gabler

Cover design: KünkelLopka GmbH, Heidelberg

Printed on acid-free paper

Springer Gabler is a brand of Springer DE. Springer DE is part of Springer Science+Business Media.
www.springer-gabler.de

Geleitwort

Cost Stickiness, zu Deutsch Kostenremanenz, stellt ein bedeutendes Controllingphänomen dar. Sie bezeichnet die empirische Beobachtung, dass Kosten bei einem Umsatzrückgang nicht in dem Maße sinken wie sie bei einem Umsatzwachstum ansteigen. In der Literatur werden hierfür vor allem zwei Gründe gesehen. Zum einen wird vermutet, dass das Management bei einem Umsatzrückgang Ressourcen beibehält, um besser auf einen zukünftigen Umsatzanstieg reagieren zu können. Dabei geht man davon aus, dass dies effizienter ist, als die Ressourcen abzubauen, um sie dann später wieder aufbauen zu müssen. Zum anderen wird argumentiert, dass das Management eine Form von Empire Building betreibt und deshalb ein hohes Ressourcenausmaß auch bei Umsatzrückgang bevorzugt. Mit dem Thema der Cost Stickiness setzt sich die vorliegende Dissertationsschrift auseinander. Neben einer Einleitung und einem Schlussteil besteht sie aus drei Hauptteilen.

Hauptteil 1 dient zum Überblick über bisherige Forschung zur Cost Stickiness. Zunächst wird hier die zentrale Studie von Anderson et al. [2003] vorgestellt. In deren Studie wird dabei auf das Verhalten der sog. SG&A Kosten (Selling, General, and Admininstrative) fokussiert. Für diese Kosten weisen Anderson et al. Cost Stickiness nach. Als mögliche Ursachen nennen sie die beiden oben erläuterten Gründe, nämlich Anpassungskosten von Ressourcen und Empire Building. Die Studie von Anderson et al. führte zu mehreren Folgestudien zur Cost Stickiness, die Baumgarten im Folgenden sehr gut strukturiert erläutert. So untersuchen bspw. einige Studien, ob Cost Stickiness auch für andere Kostenarten zutrifft und können dies bestätigen. Wiederum andere Studien untersuchen die Bedeutung des Ausmaßes der Umsatzänderung, des Zeithorizonts und des Konjunkturzyklus auf die Cost Stickiness. Ein weiterer Zweig beschäftigt sich mit firmenspezifischen Einflüssen auf Cost Stickiness, wie z.B. Anlagenintensität und Mitarbeiterintensität. In ähnlicher Weise werden branchen- und länderspezifische Eigenschaften von Cost Stickiness untersucht. Ebenfalls bedeutend sind Studien, die sich mit dem Einfluss der Manageranreize auf die Cost Stickiness beschäftigen. Baumgarten erläutert auch Studien, die sich kritisch mit dem Phänomen Cost Stickiness auseinandersetzen und zeigt inwiefern diese Kritik gerechtfertigt ist. In einem abschließenden Abschnitt werden Studien erläutert, die eine Verbindung von Cost Stickiness zu verwandten Gebieten schaffen.

In Hauptteil 2 wird das Paper „The Information Content of the SG&A Ratio" behandelt. In diesem Teil geht es darum zu unterscheiden, ob Cost Stickiness in Bezug auf die SG&A-Kosten von Unternehmen gewollt in Kauf genommen wird oder nicht. Von dieser Unterscheidung hängt es ab, ob ein Anstieg des SG&A/Sales-Ratio positive oder negative Konsequenzen besitzt. Dabei wird von einem intendierten Anstieg ausgegangen, wenn ein Unternehmen in Bezug auf das SG&A/Sales-Ratio in der Vergangenheit unter dem Branchendurchschnitt lag. Somit wird gleichsam eine Effizienzanalyse durchgeführt, die zwischen kosteneffizienten und kostenineffizienten Unternehmen unterscheidet. Mittels dieser Unterscheidung kann Baumgarten tatsächlich eine Trennung in der Wirkung von Cost Stickiness in Bezug auf die SG&A-Kosten erzielen. So zeigt sich, dass bei kosteneffizienten Firmen ein Anstieg des SG&A/Sales-Ratio intendiert zu sein scheint. Dies äußert sich in Earnings, die in Folge eines Ratio-Anstiegs ebenfalls steigen. Im Gegensatz hierzu ist ein Anstieg des Ratios bei kostenineffizienten Unternehmen als nicht intendiert anzusehen. Er hat geringere Earnings zur Folge. Weiter untermauert wird dieses interessante Ergebnis durch die Tatsache, dass der Earnings-Anstieg bei kosteneffizienten Firmen dann besonders hoch ist, wenn sie über ein hohes Verbesserungspotential in Bezug auf die Herstellungskosten verfügen. Dies deutet an, dass der Anstieg der SG&A Kosten durch gezielte Investitionen in operative Effizienz verursacht wird. Die Idee zwischen einer intendierten und nicht intendierten Cost Stickiness zu unterscheiden kann als sehr innovativ angesehen werden und ermöglicht eine neue Sichtweise auf Cost Stickiness.

Im Hauptteil 3 steht das Paper „Analysts' Implied Cost Forecasts and Cost Stickiness" im Fokus. Die Analyse basiert auf der grundlegenden Idee implizite Kostenprognosen von Analysten zu berechnen. Diese erhält man aus der Differenz von Sales- und Earnings-Prognosen. Die Eigenschaften dieser impliziten Kostenprognosen werden von Baumgarten eingehend untersucht. Zunächst wird dabei festgestellt, dass in den realen Kostendaten Cost Stickiness zu finden ist. Im Gegensatz hierzu ignorieren die impliziten Kostenprognosen hingegen Cost Stickiness. Sie sind sogar anti-sticky, d.h. bei einem Rückgang der Sales wird von einem höheren Rückgang der Kosten ausgegangen im Vergleich zum Kostenanstieg bei steigenden Sales. Dies kann als eine Inkonsistenz von Sales- und Earningsprognosen interpretiert werden. Bei einem Rückgang der Umsatzprognosen sind Analysten offensichtlich viel zu optimistisch in Bezug auf die damit einhergehenden Kosten. Baumgarten sieht den Grund hierfür darin, dass das Management die Analysten nicht ausreichend über die zukünftige Cost Stickiness informiert. Dies scheint vor allem darum plausibel, wenn man bedenkt, dass der Grund für Cost Stickiness Empire Building sein kann und das Management wenig Interesse daran hat, dies offenzulegen. Weiter zeigt Baumgarten, dass Analysten Cost Stickiness in späten Prognosen berücksichtigen, d.h. es scheint ein gewisser Lerneffekt aufzutreten. Dieser Hauptteil zeichnet sich vor allem durch die zentrale Idee aus, implizite Kostenprognosen zu berechnen, was es erlaubt zu analysieren, inwieweit Analysten reales Kostenverhalten berücksichtigen. Die Analyse zeigt, dass Analysten hier erheblichen Aufholbedarf besitzen, was ein wichtiges Ergebnis für die Verbesserung von Prognosen darstellt.

Die Arbeit kann durch den hohen Innovationsgehalt überzeugen. So werden durch zahlreiche neue Gedanken wichtige neue Ergebnisse auf dem Gebiet der Cost Stickiness erzielt. Außerdem wendet Baumgarten empirische Analysen in überzeugender Form an. Der Arbeit ist deshalb eine gute Aufnahme in der Accounting Community zu wünschen.

Prof. Dr. Carsten Homburg

Vorwort

Die vorliegende Dissertation entstand in den Jahren 2009 bis 2011 während meiner Tätigkeit als wissenschaftlicher Mitarbeiter am Seminar für Allgemeine Betriebswirtschaftslehre und Controlling der Universität zu Köln. Nach erfolgreichem Abschluss meiner Promotion möchte ich die folgenden Zeilen dafür nutzen, den Personen zu danken, die zum Gelingen des Dissertationsprojektes beigetragen haben.

Zuallererst möchte ich mich herzlich bei meinem Doktorvater und akademischen Lehrer Herrn Prof. Dr. Carsten Homburg für seine vielfältige Unterstützung und die bereichernde Zeit an seinem Seminar bedanken. Unseren persönlichen und fachlichen Austausch habe ich stets sehr geschätzt. Darüber hinaus bedanke ich mich bei Herrn Prof. Dr. Ludwig Kuntz für die Übernahme des Zweitgutachtens und bei Herrn Prof. Dr. Heinrich Schradin für die Leitung meiner Disputation. Weiterhin danke ich dem Förderverein Controlling an der Universität Köln, dessen finanzielle Unterstützung meine Präsentationen auf internationalen Forschungskonferenzen und den Zugriff auf Unternehmensdaten für meine empirischen Analysen ermöglicht hat.

Meinen Lehrstuhlkollegen Marcus Berghäuser, Sebastian Gell, Dominika Gödde, Stefan Henschke, Tanja Klettke, Michael Lorenz, Julia Nasev, Sabine Nentwig, Dominik Nußmann, Kristina Reimer und Simon Zehnder danke ich für die hervorragende Zusammenarbeit, die fruchtbaren Diskussionen und die schöne gemeinsame Zeit. Besonderer Dank gilt meinen Kollegen Christian Müller und Philipp Plank, deren Freundschaft ein wertvoller Gewinn aus meiner Promotionszeit ist, und insbesondere Ute Bonenkamp und Max Berens, die mir während der intensiven Arbeit an gemeinsamen Forschungsprojekten sehr ans Herz gewachsen sind. Weiterer Dank gilt den studentischen Hilfskräften des Lehrstuhls für ihre unermüdlichen Unterstützungsangebote. Besonders hervorzuheben ist dabei das Team der Lehrstuhl-IT: Norman Franke, Dennis Hoppius, Heiko Limbach, Martin Müller und Adrian Porger, deren 24/7-Mentalität stets einen reibungslosen EDV-Betrieb ermöglicht hat. Dank sagen möchte ich ebenso Elisabeth Tokarski-Eich, die als Sekretärin und „Mutter der Kompanie" jederzeit für ein kollegiales und harmonisches Klima am Seminar sorgt.

Vor allem möchte ich meiner Frau Magdalene, meinen Eltern Margot und Axel sowie meinen Geschwistern Sylvia und Christoph danken. Mit ihrer liebevollen Unterstützung haben Sie mir ein Umfeld geschenkt, das von Lebensfreude und Zuversicht erfüllt ist. Danke für alles!

Daniel Baumgarten

Table of Contents

List of Figures

List of Tables

List of Abbreviations

AAA	American Accounting Association
ABC	Activity-based costing
ABJ	Anderson, Banker, and Janakiraman (Anderson et al. [2003])
adj.	adjusted
CEO	Chief executive officer
COGS	Cost of goods sold
CRSP	Center for Research in Security Prices
CSHOQ	Monthly common shares outstanding
e.g.	for example ("exempli gratia")
EBIT	Earnings before interest and taxes
EPS	Earnings per share
et al.	and others ("et alii")
FIFO	First in, first out
GDP	Gross domestic product
H	Hypothesis
I/B/E/S	Institutional Brokers' Estimate System
i.e.	that is ("id est")
IT	Information technology
LIFO	Last in, first out
M&A	Mergers and acquisitions
OECD	Organisation for Economic Co-operation and Development
OLS	Ordinary least squares
PCM	Proportionate cost model
PRCCM	Monthly share price
R&D	Research and development
SG&A	Selling, general, and administrative
SIC	Standard Industrial Classification
UK	United Kingdom

US	United States
US-GAAP	United States Generally Accepted Accounting Principles
USA	United States of America
vif	Variance inflation factor
vs.	versus
WRDS	Wharton Research Data Services

List of Symbols

Latin Symbols

$Accounts\ Receivables_{i,t}$	Accounts receivables of firm *i* in year *t*
$AQ_{i,t}$	Audit qualification of firm *i* in year *t*
$AR_{i,t}$	Change in the ratio of accounts receivables to sales of firm *i* in year *t*
C_0	Current cost level
$CAPX_{i,t}$	Change in the ratio of capital expenditure of firm *i* in year *t* to the average change in firm *i*'s industry in year *t*
$CEPS_{i,t}$	Change in earnings per share of firm *i* in year *t* deflated by the share price of firm *i* at the end of year *t*-1
$CEPS1_{i,t+1}$	Change in earnings per share of firm *i* in year *t*+1 deflated by the share price of firm *i* at the end of year *t*
$COEPS_{i,t}$	Change in operating earnings per share of firm *i* in year *t* deflated by the share price of firm *i* at the end of year *t*-1
$COEPS1_{i,t+1}$	Change in operating earnings per share of firm *i* in year *t*+1 deflated by the share price of firm *i* at the end of year *t*
$COGS_{i,t}$	Cost of goods sold of firm *i* in year *t*
$Costs_{i,t}$	Actual total costs of firm *i* in year *t*
$\widehat{Costs}_{i,t}$	Analysts' implied cost forecast for firm *i* in year *t*
$D^{saleincr}_{i,t}$	Dummy variable indicating a sales increase of firm *i* in year *t*
$D^{sga\_low}_{i,t}$	Dummy variable indicating cost efficiency of firm *i* in year *t*-1
$Decrease\_Dummy_{i,t}$	Dummy variable indicating an increase in (actual) sales of firm *i* in year *t*
$\widehat{Decrease\_Dummy}_{i,t}$	Dummy variable indicating analysts' forecast of a sales increase for firm *i* in year *t*
$Earnings_{i,t}$	Actual earnings of firm *i* in year *t*
$\widehat{Earnings}_{i,t}$	Analysts' earnings forecast for firm *i* in year *t*
$Earnings\ per\ share_{i,t}$	Earnings per share of firm *i* in year *t*

$EBT_{i,t}$	Earnings before taxes of firm *i* in year *t*
$Employees_{i,t}$	Number of employees of firm *i* in year *t*
$EQ_{i,t}$	Earnings quality of firm *i* in year *t*
$Equity_{i,t}$	Equity of firm *i* in year *t*
$ETR_{i,t}$	Change in the effective tax rate of firm *i* in year *t*
$FEear_{i,t}$	Earnings forecast error of firm *i* in year *t*
$FEsal_{i,t}$	Sales forecast error of firm *i* in year *t*
$GM_{i,t}$	Change in the ratio of gross margin to sales of firm *i* in year *t*
$Gross\ Margin_{i,t}$	Gross margin of firm *i* in year *t*
$Growth_{i,t}$	Change in sales growth of firm *i* in year *t*
$Firm\ Capital\ Expenditure_{i,t}$	Capital expenditure of firm *i* in year *t*
i	Firm index
$Industry\ Capital\ Expenditure_{i,t}$	Average capital expenditure of firm *i*'s industry in year *t*
INT	Intercept of a regression
$INV_{i,t}$	Change in the ratio of inventory to sales of firm *i* in year *t*
$Inventory_{i,t}$	Inventory of firm *i* in year *t*
j	Index for control variables
$LEV_{i,t}$	Change in leverage of firm *i* in year *t*
$LF_{i,t}$	Relative change in the ratio of sales per employee of firm *i* in year *t*
$\log[...]$	Logarithm of [...]
$Long\text{-}term\ Debt_{i,t}$	Long-term debt of firm *i* in year *t*
$Marketcap_{i,t-1}$	Market capitalization of firm *i* in year *t*-1
N	Number of observations
$Operating\ Earnings\ per\ Share_{i,t}$	Operating earnings per share of firm *i* in year *t*
$Other\ Signals_{i,j,t}$	Control variable *j* of firm *i* in year *t*
$P_{i,t-1}$	Share price of firm *i* at the end of fiscal year *t*-1

Q1	Lower quartile
Q3	Upper quartile
R^2	Coefficient of determination of a regression
S_0	Current sales level
$Sales_{i,t}$	(Actual) sales of firm *i* in year *t*
$\widehat{Sales}_{i,t}$	Analysts' sales forecast for firm *i* in year *t*
$SG\&A_{i,t}$	Selling, general, and administrative costs of firm *i* in year *t*
$SG\&A_{i,t}^{sales\_fall}$	Change in the ratio of selling, general, and administrative costs to sales of firm *i* in year *t* if sales of firm *i* decrease in *t*
$SG\&A_{i,t}^{sales\_rise}$	Change in the ratio of selling, general, and administrative costs to sales of firm *i* in year *t* if sales of firm *i* increase in *t*
$SG\&A_{i,t}^{sga\_high}$	Change in the ratio of selling, general, and administrative costs to sales of firm *i* in year *t* if this ratio of firm *i* was above the industry average in *t*-1
$SG\&A_{i,t}^{sga\_low}$	Change in the ratio of selling, general, and administrative costs to sales of firm *i* in year *t* if this ratio of firm *i* was below or equal to the industry average in *t*-1
$SG\&A_{i,t}^{sga\_high\_cogs\_high}$	Change in the ratio of selling, general, and administrative costs to sales of firm *i* in year *t* if this ratio of firm *i* was above the industry average in *t*-1 and the ratio of cost of goods sold to sales of firm *i* was above the industry average in *t*-1
$SG\&A_{i,t}^{sga\_high\_cogs\_low}$	Change in the ratio of selling, general, and administrative costs to sales of firm *i* in year *t* if this ratio of firm *i* was above the industry average in *t*-1 and the ratio of cost of goods sold to sales of firm *i* was below or equal to the industry average in *t*-1
$SG\&A_{i,t}^{sga\_low\_cogs\_high}$	Change in the ratio of selling, general, and administrative costs to sales of firm *i* in year *t* if this ratio of firm *i* was below or equal to the industry average in *t*-1 and the ratio of cost of goods sold to sales of firm *i* was above the industry average in *t*-1

$SG\&A_{i,t}^{sga\_low\_cogs\_low}$	Change in the ratio of selling, general, and administrative costs to sales of firm *i* in year *t* if this ratio of firm *i* was below or equal to the industry average in *t*-1 and the ratio of cost of goods sold to sales of firm *i* was below or equal to the industry average in *t*-1
$SG\&A\ Signal_{i,t}$	Change in the ratio of selling, general, and administrative costs to sales of firm *i* in year *t*
t	(End of) year *t*
$Tax\ Expense_{i,t}$	Tax expense of firm *i* in year *t*
$Tax\ Rate_{i,t}$	Tax rate of firm *i* in year *t*

Greek Symbols

α	Regression coefficient or intercept
β	Regression coefficient or intercept
γ	Regression coefficient
δ	Regression coefficient
ε	Error term, residual of a regression
$\sum_{j=1}^{J}[...]$	Sum of [...] for j=1 to J
τ	Running time index

Further Symbol

#	(Item) number

1 Introduction

The analysis and prediction of cost behavior is clearly relevant to accounting researchers, managers, financial analysts, and professional investors, since all these groups rely fundamentally on cost accounting data for their core work activities. According to traditional models of cost behavior, as presented in accounting textbooks, costs are considered to be either fixed or variable with respect to changes in the activity level of a firm.[1] By definition, at least in the short run, fixed costs are independent of the level of activity. Variable costs, by contrast, are commonly considered to change symmetrically or even proportionally with changes in activity. This implies that the extent of a change in variable costs depends only on the extent of the simultaneous change in activity level and not on the direction of the change.

However, over the past two decades, a rising number of accounting research studies has documented an asymmetric cost response to changes in activity level.[2] Costs turn out to decrease less when activity falls than they increase when activity rises. Anderson et al. [2003] are the first to thoroughly analyze this asymmetric cost behavior, which they (and subsequent research studies) refer to as "cost stickiness", in a comprehensive empirical study that focuses on the behavior of selling, general, and administrative (SG&A) costs. Deviating from the traditional textbook models of cost behavior, Anderson et al. [2003] introduce an alternative model in which costs do not change mechanically with simultaneous changes in activity, but rather due to deliberate resource adjustment decisions made by managers. Anderson et al. [2003] identify two major causes of sticky cost behavior, namely adjustment costs and personal considerations by self-interested managers. The rationale underlying the theory of adjustment costs as a driver of cost stickiness is the following. When the demand for the products and services of a firm declines, managers can either retain redundant resources and bear the associated costs, or they can cut the redundant resources and bear the resulting adjustment costs. If the decline in demand is only temporary, the adjustment costs of reducing resources and ramping them up soon

---

1 See, e.g., Garrison et al. [2009].

2 Examples of these studies include Malcom [1991], Banker and Johnston [1993], Mak and Roush [1994], Noreen and Soderstrom [1994, 1997], and West [2003]. See Chapter 2 for further details. Earlier research in the field already occasionally documented patterns which are consistent with asymmetric cost responses, such as descriptions of cost behavior referred to as "*Kostenremanenz*" in German research literature (see, e.g., Strube [1936]).

afterwards is likely to exceed the costs of temporarily retaining redundant resources. Adjustment costs of reducing resources may include the selling costs of firm-specific assets, severance payments to dismissed employees, and further penalties resulting from breach of contract. Additionally, adjustment costs also include those associated with adding resources when demand recovers, such as customization costs for new firm-specific assets, search and training costs for new employees, or negotiation costs for future contracts. Thus, costs are considered not only to be driven by the current sales level, but also by managerial expectations of future sales. The rationale underlying the theory of personal considerations by self-interested managers as a driver of cost stickiness is that managers do not always make decisions that result in the best outcome for the firm's shareholders. Instead, managers tend to maximize their own utility and therefore may be reluctant to reduce resources, in order to avoid a loss of status and power.

As the first of three contributions, my doctoral thesis provides the first structured and comprehensive review of currently existing research on sticky cost behavior. In this review, I emphasize supporting and conflicting findings and reveal promising potential for future research. Since 2003, a wide range of accounting research studies has built on the cost stickiness concept and analyzed various characteristics of asymmetric cost behavior and their variation at the firm, industry, and country-level. Most of these studies focus on the influence of specific factors on the level of adjustment costs which, in turn, are considered to determine the extent of sticky cost behavior. Apart from that, several studies also shed light on the impact of managerial incentives that induce managers either to delay resource reductions or to more readily adjust costs to the current level of demand. Additionally, a few accounting research studies criticize the prevailing approach of measuring cost stickiness and the validity of the assumed underlying causes. Finally, a small number of research studies apply the cost stickiness concept to related financial research areas, such as conditional conservatism or audit fees. Considering that several years have elapsed since Anderson et al. [2003] emphasized the relevance of their findings for related areas and also bearing in mind the relatively large number of follow-up studies,[3] research combining cost stickiness with that on related areas appears rather small. This research gap is also highlighted by Weiss [2010] and Banker et al. [2011c, 14] who, for instance, state that

[3] More specifically, Anderson et al. [2003, 62] discuss the implications for financial forecasts, auditing, and financial statement analysis.

"(...) most of the empirical literature on sticky costs focus on characterizing various aspects of sticky cost behavior. However, much less attention has been paid to the important implications of sticky costs for other areas." I aim to fill this research gap by providing two large-scale empirical analyses as the second and third major contributions of this doctoral thesis. In these comprehensive studies, I present several significant implications of sticky cost behavior for fundamental analysis and for financial analysts' forecasts.

In the first study, I analyze cost stickiness in conjunction with the information content of the SG&A ratio, that is, the ratio of selling, general, and administrative costs to sales. An increase in this important key figure is associated with contradictory interpretations, namely a negative one due to deficient cost control and a positive one derived primarily from cost stickiness (see Anderson et al. [2007]). Based on these conflicting explanations, I argue that it is crucial to distinguish between whether or not an increase in the ratio of SG&A costs to sales is actually *intended* by management, in order to enhance future profitability. I regard an increase as intended if a company's past SG&A ratio was below its industry average, representing efficiency in SG&A cost management. Indeed, these intended increases significantly enhance future earnings. I attribute this positive impact to lower future cost of goods sold and demonstrate that this effect is particularly strong if there is substantial latitude for reducing these costs. This finding suggests that intended SG&A expenditures partially represent investments in operating efficiency. In my analysis, I elaborate on Anderson et al.'s [2007] study which examines the impact of cost stickiness on the interpretation of an increase in the SG&A ratio and compare their approach to my differentiation in terms of cost efficiency. This comparison reveals a more significant, stronger, and more persistent signaling effect in the case of my segmentation. In addition, my approach has explanatory power that is incremental to the differentiation based on sticky cost behavior.

All in all, this study provides important implications for managers through presenting a benchmarking approach for assessing SG&A investments. Additionally, I present implications for external users of financial statements, such as capital market investors and analysts, with respect to evaluating changes in the SG&A ratio beyond the prevailing interpretation.

The second large-scale study presented in this doctoral thesis combines cost stickiness with financial analysts' forecasts and shows that analysts do not consider cost stickiness when forming their expectations of future cost behavior. More specifically, I find that analysts' implied cost forecasts (the differences between forecasted sales and forecasted earnings) disregard cost stickiness. I attribute this finding to a previously unexplored form of optimism in analysts' earnings forecasts. Analysts' earnings forecasts are not only "externally" optimistic, i.e., too high with respect to actual earnings, but also "internally" optimistic, that is, too high with respect to forecasted sales. I argue that one of the main drivers of internal optimism is analysts' reliance on managerial information. Managers dislike being regarded as self-interested or inefficient. Consequently, when sales are expected to fall, managers promise analysts unrealistically high resource cuts, rather than disclose their tendency to retain redundant resources due to status considerations. Analysts who rely on managerial information then issue earnings forecasts that are too high with respect to the expected sales decrease.

The results of my second study are of interest to both analysts and investors. Analysts can take advantage of my findings by becoming more aware of cost behavior and its underlying managerial incentives. If they ensure that their forecasts reflect the stickiness that characterizes actual cost behavior, they can increase the consistency and accuracy of their earnings and sales forecasts. Similarly, investors can benefit from my results by critically checking analysts' earnings and sales forecasts for consistency with cost stickiness, before they use these forecasts as a basis for investment decisions.

All in all, my doctoral thesis comprehensively analyzes the cost stickiness phenomenon by discussing its development and all relevant findings presented in the research literature. Furthermore, the thesis contains several suggestions for future research and discusses important implications of cost stickiness for fundamental analysis and analysts' forecasts by means of two comprehensive empirical analyses.

The doctoral thesis is structured as follows. In Chapter 2, I present the cost stickiness phenomenon in detail by outlining the development of the research field and discussing the complete existing research literature. In Chapter 3, I analyze the information content of cost stickiness for the interpretation of the SG&A ratio, an important key figure in fundamental analysis, and present an alternative approach to differentiate between positive and negative effects of an increase in this ratio. In Chapter 4, I combine cost stickiness with financial analysts' forecasts and show that analysts generally disregard the stickiness of costs when determining their forecasts. In

Chapter 5, I summarize the main results and findings and indicate useful directions for future research. Figure 1.1 depicts the structure of the thesis.

Figure 1.1: Structure of the Doctoral Thesis

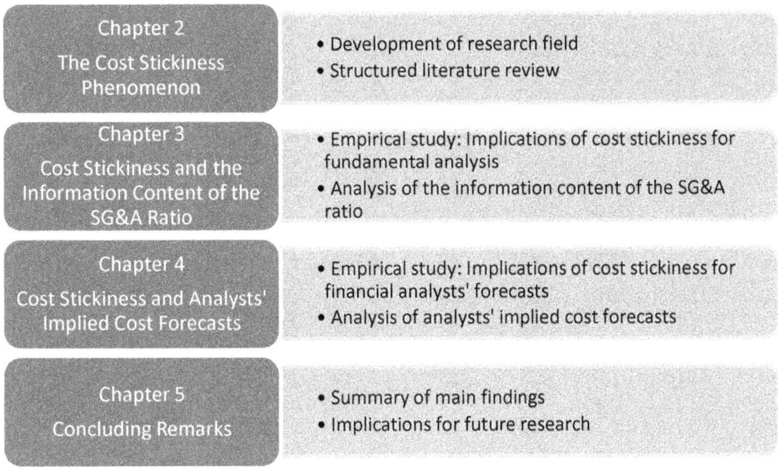

2 The Cost Stickiness Phenomenon

This chapter provides the framework for the subsequent ones and reveals potential for future research through a comprehensive discussion of the cost stickiness phenomenon. Section 2.1 differentiates between sticky cost behavior and the traditional assumption of symmetric or proportional changes in costs in response to changes in activity. For this purpose, Section 2.1 first presents the main findings from several research studies that provide early indications of an asymmetric reaction of costs to changes in activity. Furthermore, Section 2.1 discusses the seminal study of Anderson et al. [2003], which links cost stickiness to deliberate managerial behavior and laid the groundwork for cost stickiness as a distinct field of research. Section 2.2 discusses and structures the existing research literature on the characteristics of cost stickiness. The discussion of these studies is divided into several subsections, each of which has an individual focus and explores either general, firm-specific, industry-specific, or country-specific characteristics of cost stickiness. Section 2.3 elaborates on studies analyzing the impact of managerial incentives on sticky cost behavior. Section 2.4 discusses studies that challenge the validity of the established approach of measuring cost stickiness and the assumed underlying causes, as well as a study that responds to such criticism. Section 2.5 presents research studies that apply the cost stickiness concept to related financial research areas. Thus, Section 2.5 serves as a bridge to my subsequent analysis, which yields various implications of sticky cost behavior for fundamental analysis and financial analysts' forecasts, as presented in Chapters 3 and 4. Figure 2.1 depicts the structure of Chapter 2.

Figure 2.1: Structure of Chapter 2

2.1 Evidence on the Stickiness of Costs and its Potential Causes

2.2 Characteristics of Cost Stickiness

2.3 Cost Stickiness and Managerial Incentives

2.4 Criticism of the Cost Stickiness Concept

2.5 Application of the Cost Stickiness Concept to Related Financial Research

2.1 Evidence on the Stickiness of Costs and its Potential Causes

According to the traditional assumption in cost accounting, costs are either fixed (step-fixed) or variable with respect to changes in the activity level of a firm. By definition, at least in the short run, *fixed* costs are independent of the level of activity. The relationship between *variable* costs and activity changes, by contrast, is commonly considered to be symmetric or even proportional to increases and decreases in activity.[4] *Symmetric* changes in costs require that costs change to the same extent, regardless of the direction of a given change in activity. Under this assumption, costs that, for instance, increase by 0.7 percent per one percent increase in sales also decrease by 0.7 percent per one percent decrease in sales. The assumption of *proportional* changes in costs goes even further and requires that a one percent increase in activity results in a one percent increase in costs and that a one percent decrease in activity results in a one percent decrease in costs.[5]

Early research in the field already occasionally challenged the traditional view of costs responding symmetrically or proportionally to activity changes and described patterns in which changes in costs depend not only on the magnitude of a change in activity, but also on the direction of the change.[6] However, from the early nineties onwards, various research studies consistently report that costs tend not to change symmetrically or proportionally with changes in activity. For instance, in his study on overhead costs in activity-based costing systems, Malcom [1991, 76] observes that "many of these new costs tend to be somewhat nonvariable in character, i.e., lumpy and not strictly proportional to activity (…) these lumpy costs stick even if activity declines (…)." In a discussion of Malcom's [1991] study, Mak and Roush [1994, 97] state that "'Sticky' costs may increase in the short term, but do not decrease with a decline in activity in the short term." In a further study, Banker and Johnston [1993] find that changes in costs are not exclusively determined by changes in output volume or capacity and suggest that additional important drivers should be identified. Noreen

4 Symmetric or proportional changes in variable costs with respect to changes in activity are an underlying assumption of both accounting textbooks and research studies. See Garrison et al. [2009] for an accounting textbook example. As one example presenting the prevalent view in a research study, Noreen [1991, 162] points out that in "the typical cost system found in practice (…) all allocation bases (e.g., activity measures) are proportional to volume."

5 See, e.g., Calleja et al. [2006, 128].

6 As an example, observations which are consistent with sticky cost behavior were already described in German research literature as early as 1936 (see Strube [1936]). An early description of sticky cost behavior in US research literature can, for instance, be found in Beyer [1963].

and Soderstrom [1994] empirically address the question of whether overhead costs move strictly proportionally with activity. For a sample of hospitals from Washington State, Noreen and Soderstrom [1994, 273-274] reject the hypothesis that overhead costs change strictly proportionally with activity for most analyzed cost accounts. The authors point out that this result is crucial for the application of various standard cost accounting methods. In a follow-up study, Noreen and Soderstrom [1997, 90] arrive at similar conclusions that "cost systems which assume costs are strictly proportional to activity (such as conventional or ABC systems) grossly overstate the impact of activity on costs." Furthermore, Noreen and Soderstrom [1997, 96-97] find that only about 30 percent of overhead costs change with activity, and they also provide moderate evidence that "costs change more readily in response to increases in activity than to decreases in activity." Thus, Noreen and Soderstrom already observe cost stickiness. However, they do not expand on potential causes of such cost behavior. Cooper and Kaplan [1998] fill this gap and provide some initial anecdotal evidence of the influence of deliberate managerial decisions on sticky cost behavior. More precisely, Cooper and Kaplan [1998, 247] state: "Thus, what makes a resource cost 'variable' in a downward direction is not inherent in the nature of the resource; it is a function of management decisions–first to reduce the demands for the resource, and second, to lower the spending on the resource."

In their seminal study, Anderson et al. [2003] (hereafter referred to as "ABJ") build on these prior indications of asymmetry in cost reaction with respect to activity increases and decreases. ABJ introduce the term "cost stickiness", by showing that selling, general, and administrative (SG&A) costs decrease less when sales fall than they increase when sales rise.[7] This emerged from a large-scale empirical analysis, including firm-year data over a 20-year-period. As the major contribution of this study, ABJ explain cost stickiness in terms of managerial behavior, that is, managers who deliberately adjust resources in response to changes in activity. In this context, ABJ [2003, 49-50] identify two major reasons why managers may be reluctant to cut redundant resourses when activity declines and thus respond asymmetrically to increases and decreases in activity, namely adjustment costs and personal considerations by self-interested managers.

[7] In addition to the discretionary character of SG&A costs, ABJ [2003, 48] specifically analyze this cost type due to its wide availability in the Compustat database and its relation to sales as an appropriate proxy for changes in the activity level. Moreover, SG&A costs represent an important cost type, comprising over 26% of average sales revenue in ABJ's sample.

Firstly, *adjustment costs* are a potential cause of cost stickiness, because, when demand declines, managers are faced with a trade-off between the costs of retaining redundant resources on the one hand, and resource-adjustment costs on the other. Retaining redundant resources incurs costs if firm resources are maintained at a higher level than would be necessary to meet the current level of demand. Adjustment costs are incurred if firm resources are adapted to the new lower level of activity. Adjustment costs may include the selling costs of firm-specific assets, severance payments to dismissed employees, and further penalties resulting from breach of contract. Apart from monetary costs, adjustment costs may also be indirect, such as a decline in morale or loyalty among the remaining workforce. Additionally, adjustment costs also include those associated with adding resources when demand recovers, such as customization costs for new firm-specific assets, search and training costs for new employees, or negotiation costs for future contracts.[8] If managers expect a decrease in activity to be only temporary, the costs of reducing resources and ramping them up soon afterwards is likely to exceed the costs of temporarily retaining redundant resources. Thus, cost stickiness may be attributed to manager intentions to maximize long-term firm value by avoiding unnecessarily high future adjustment costs. ABJ and various follow-up studies confirm the validity of this assumption by providing empirical evidence of an intensifying effect of several factors that increase the level of firm-specific adjustment costs on cost stickiness. These studies and their implications are presented in Section 2.2.

Secondly, *personal considerations by self-interested managers* are a potential cause of cost stickiness, because previous research shows that self-interested managers strive to maximize their personal utility, instead of making decisions that lead to the best outcome for the firm's shareholders (see, e.g., Jensen and Meckling [1976]). These personal considerations result in agency costs when self-interested managers omit necessary resource reductions, in order to avoid a loss of status or the anguish of dismissing familiar employees. Research studies on the impact of managerial incentives on the sticky behavior of costs are presented in Section 2.3. Indeed, various follow-up studies provide comprehensive evidence of both major causes of cost stickiness identified by ABJ, namely adjustment costs and personal considerations by self-interested managers.

---

[8] See ABJ [2003, 49].

ABJ [2003, 52] test for sticky cost behavior by introducing an empirical model that analyzes the relation between changes in SG&A costs and simultaneous changes in sales. The model specification is the following:

$$\log\left[\frac{SG\&A_{i,t}}{SG\&A_{i,t-1}}\right]=\beta_0+\beta_1\cdot\log\left[\frac{Sales_{i,t}}{Sales_{i,t-1}}\right]+\beta_2\cdot Decrease\_Dummy_{i,t}\cdot\log\left[\frac{Sales_{i,t}}{Sales_{i,t-1}}\right]+\varepsilon_{i,t} \qquad [2.1]$$

$SG\&A_{i,t}$ ($SG\&A_{i,t-1}$) and $Sales_{i,t}$ ($Sales_{i,t-1}$) represent the SG&A costs and sales of firm *i* in year *t* (*t*-1), respectively. In order to distinguish between periods of rising and falling sales, the model includes an interaction dummy variable $Decrease\_Dummy_{i,t}$ that takes the value one if the sales of firm *i* decrease between periods *t*-1 and *t*, and zero otherwise. Due to the log-specification of the model, the coefficient values can easily be interpreted as percentage changes in SG&A costs and sales. Consequently, the coefficient β_1 measures the average percentage increase in SG&A costs for a one percent increase in sales, while the sum of β_1 and β_2 measures the average percentage decrease for a one percent decrease in sales. If the SG&A costs are indeed sticky, the increase in SG&A costs when sales rise should exceed the decrease in SG&A costs when sales fall by an equivalent amount. Therefore, the empirical expectation for model [2.1] is a significantly negative value for β_2, given a positive value for β_1.

ABJ [2003, 53-55] estimate their cost stickiness model using OLS regression and find that SG&A costs, on average, increase by 0.55 percent per one percent increase in sales, and decrease by only 0.35 percent per one percent decrease in sales. This result of significant SG&A cost stickiness proves to be robust when applying several alternative estimation approaches, such as a linear model instead of the log-linear specification or a time-series estimation of individual firms instead of the analysis of panel data. Almost all follow-up studies presented in Sections 2.2 to 2.5 utilize the model specification of ABJ. However, they occasionally modify or extend the model with respect to their specific research questions.[9]

Taken together, ABJ provide the first large-scale empirical evidence on the prevalence of SG&A cost stickiness. However, the greatest impact of ABJ's study on subsequent research lies in the explanation of cost stickiness in terms of an alternative

9 A typical modification of ABJ's model within their own study and in various follow-up studies is the inclusion of additional factors, such as asset and employee intensity, in the form of interaction terms, into the model. This approach allows for an analysis of the impact of these factors on the β_2 coefficient, which determines the difference in the cost reaction to rising and falling sales, that is, in the level of cost stickiness.

model of cost behavior. In this model, costs do not move mechanically with changes in activity, but are deliberately adjusted by managers. Concerning ABJ's contribution, Anderson and Lanen [2009, 3], for instance, "believe that it is the connection to cost management that is of interest to most researchers." Previous studies finding indications of sticky cost patterns in their respective data often attribute this observation exclusively to inefficient cost control, rather than to deliberate managerial behavior. Just as one example, West [2003, 14-15] states that "costs are more sticky when managers have less control over costs relative to volume."

Since 2003, a wide range of accounting research studies has extended and developed the cost stickiness concept. The subsequent sections of this chapter present the research questions and conclusions of these follow-up studies, focusing on the characteristics, causes, and implications of the sticky behavior of costs.

2.2 Characteristics of Cost Stickiness

The seminal study of ABJ resulted in various follow-up studies analyzing different characteristics of cost stickiness. These studies consider different factors influencing the stickiness of costs and provide further insight into the drivers and consequences of this cost phenomenon. The following section provides a comprehensive overview of current research on cost stickiness, highlighting both supporting and conflicting findings. This overview is organized according to the particular characteristics of cost stickiness, rather than by study. Thus, several studies are referred to several times in different subsections, if they address different characteristics.

2.2.1 General Characteristic of Cost Stickiness

2.2.1.1 Stickiness of Different Cost Components

While several cost-stickiness-related studies follow the original one of ABJ and focus exclusively on the sticky behavior of *SG&A costs*, some studies adapt ABJ's approach to other cost categories or use more aggregated cost definitions. These analyses reveal whether other cost types are also affected by sticky behavior. The adaptation of the analysis of sticky costs to other cost types is also important in order to rule out potential distortions caused by the discretionary allocation of costs to different categories. In particular, managers can, within certain limits, make use of leeway in the classification of costs to SG&A costs and cost of goods sold (COGS). Dieckmann and White [2005, 20] highlight this potential distortion by pointing out that "there are many examples of companies playing the SG&A 'shell game' by moving expenses and resourses to COGS from SG&A and vice versa."

As one of the first follow-up studies, Subramaniam and Weidenmier [2003] apply the research design of ABJ to COGS, instead of SG&A costs, and also to the sum of these two types of costs. Subramaniam and Weidenmier [2003, 12-13] find sticky behavior of SG&A costs and COGS, both *individually* and *jointly*. Empirical evidence of the stickiness of COGS is also found by Kajiwara and Yasukata [2011, 18] for a sample of Japanese companies. Banker et al. [2006a, 21 and 2011d, 36-38] additionally find stickiness of total SG&A costs, advertising costs, research and development costs, other SG&A costs, and COGS. In addition, Banker and Chen [2006a, 25], as well as Calleja et al. [2006, 133-135], provide evidence of stickiness of total operating costs (the sum of SG&A and COGS) for various samples of international firms. Moreover, Dierynck and Renders [2009, 21-22] provide empirical evidence of labor cost stickiness. Anderson et al. [2005, 14-18] analyze the behavior of different types of discretionary costs at Southwest Airlines and find significant stickiness of operations costs, but not of labor and stations costs. Hey et al. [2011] modify the methodology introduced by ABJ to show that audit fees are also sticky.[10] All in all, many different studies demonstrate that the cost stickiness phenomenon is not limited to SG&A costs, but rather affects several cost types in various contexts.

While the research studies mentioned above examine differences in sticky cost behavior at the *firm level*, only two studies consider variations in cost stickiness at the *department level* within a firm. This is due mainly to limited data availability. In their study on the short-term cost behavior of Ontario hospitals, Balakrishnan and Gruca [2008] analyze within-firm variation in the stickiness of operating costs. Therefore, they distinguish between the costs of activities related to the hospital's core competency (patient care) on the one hand and the costs of ancillary services (e.g., administration, laundry, or dietetics) on the other. Balakrishnan and Gruca [2008,

---

[10] Instead of changes in sales as drivers of cost changes, Hey et al.'s [2011] study of audit fee stickiness applies changes in established drivers of audit fees. These drivers are: Total assets, number of unique business segments, ratio of current assets to total assets, ratio of long-term debt to total assets, ratio of EBIT to total assets, income derived from foreign operations, and a loss in the current or any of the previous two years.

1002] find empirical evidence of cost stickiness only for activities that are closely related to patient care. They argue that this result can be attributed to higher adjustment costs for resources supporting patient care, compared to those supporting ancillary services. In a follow-up study, Balakrishnan and Soderstrom [2008, 14] arrive at the same conclusions for a sample of Californian short-term general care hospitals. Consequently, typical drivers of sticky costs, such as the level of associated adjustment costs, appear to affect the extent of cost stickiness not only between firms, but also between different divisions within a firm. Future research on cost stickiness could build on this finding by conducting an intra-firm analysis in a competitive industry outside the health sector.

2.2.1.2 The Influence of the Magnitude of Changes in Activity

According to the reasoning of ABJ and various follow-up studies, the firm-specific degree of cost stickiness depends decisively on managerial expectations of the intensity and persistence of a current demand drop.[11] If managers expect a temporary decline in demand, bearing the costs of idle capacity is preferable to hastily reducing resources and costly ramping them up soon afterwards. Managerial assessment of the seriousness and duration of a demand shift, in turn, should depend on the *magnitude* of the change in activity. In contrast to minor changes in activity, major activity changes may force managers to adjust the cost structure of the firm more promptly.

Subramaniam and Weidenmier [2003] address this notion and re-estimate the regression analysis of ABJ, while distinguishing between six bands of relative changes in activity. These bands cover changes in sales within a range of five percent each, starting with changes between zero and five percent in the first band, up to changes between 25 and 30 percent in the sixth band.[12] Subramaniam and Weidenmier [2003, 11-13] find no indications of cost stickiness for minor decreases in sales, which are supposed to induce managers to retain resources until the drop in demand proves to be enduring. By contrast, when sales decrease by more than ten percent, SG&A costs as well as COGS are significantly sticky.

---

[11] See Section 2.1.

[12] Changes in sales above 30 percent are excluded, in order to remove effects caused by M&A and bankruptcy.

In contrast to this finding, Balakrishnan et al. [2004, 295-297] find no differences in cost reactions to changes in activity of either less than or more than three percent. This conflicting result might be attributed to the fact that Balakrishnan et al. [2004] analyze changes in the activity level of US physical therapy clinics, measured by therapist hours and salary paid to therapists. These changes in activity might be incomparable to changes in sales of a manufacturing firm. Also in direct contrast to the unexpected finding of Subramaniam and Weidenmier [2003], Calleja et al. [2006, 135] find lower stickiness if sales drop by more than 10 percent. This finding suggests that the sticky behavior of costs is associated with small changes in activity, which do not necessarily trigger managerial reactions such as contract renegotiations.

2.2.1.3 The Time Horizon of Cost Stickiness

ABJ [2003, 50] argue that the occurrence of cost stickiness in a single period reflects the costs of resources that have become redundant due to a drop in demand for products and services. However, if the observation period is extended to two or more years, the persistence of a demand drop becomes more certain and adjustment costs decrease relatively compared to the costs of retaining redundant resources. Consequently, cost stickiness is assumed to be lower if a longer time horizon is considered. Indeed, ABJ [2003, 55-56] find less cost stickiness if the underlying accounting data is measured over a time period longer than one year. A longer observation period should be associated with more information on the persistence and causes of a decline in demand, leading to more appropriate adjustment decisions.

The same cost behavior is observed by He et al. [2010, 7-8] for Japanese firms. Calleja et al. [2006, 135] also find lower operating cost stickiness for firms in the USA, UK, and France, if the cost stickiness model is extended to a two-year period. However, a decline in cost stickiness over a longer observation period cannot be confirmed for a subsample of German firms. Furthermore, Hay et al. [2011, 15] also provide empirical evidence of a decrease in sticky behavior over longer time periods in their analysis of audit fee stickiness. All in all, a significant decline in cost stickiness when the observation window is expanded appears to prevail for different countries and cost types.

2.2.1.4 *Cyclical Characteristics of Cost Stickiness*

ABJ [2003, 51] point out that managers not only consider firm-specific factors contributing to a decline in demand, but also measures of *economic development* in their specific product market and in the economy as a whole. When substantial economic growth is expected, managers are more likely to consider a decline in demand to be temporary, than when low or negative economic growth seems likely. These positive managerial expectations, in conjunction with higher costs of replacing laid off employees due to a shortage of skilled workforce during growth periods, may lead to greater cost stickiness. ABJ [2003, 61] indeed find a significantly positive effect of GDP growth on cost stickiness, consistent with the notion that managers consider a decline in sales to be more transitory "in a strong economic climate."

Calleja et al. [2006] also confirm a higher degree of cost stickiness during times of strong economic growth for their sample of international firms. By dividing their sample into two 5-year periods of high economic growth (1988-1993 and 1994-1999) and one 5-year period of low economic growth (2000-2004), Calleja et al. [2006, 133] find the highest level of cost stickiness during the period with the highest rate of growth. Furthermore, He et al. [2010, 8-9] analyze the sticky behavior of costs before and after the asset bubble burst in Japan in 1992. During the lengthy recession in Japan after 1992, managers were under greater pressure to promptly reduce excess capacity and become more flexible by the use of outsourcing and a contingent workforce. These factors resulted in less sticky costs in the post-bubble decade compared to prior years.

2.2.2 Firm-Specific Characteristics of Cost Stickiness

According to the reasoning of ABJ [2003, 50], during periods of weak demand, managers face a trade-off between bearing the costs of retaining redundant resources and bearing the adjustment costs of reducing resources and ramping them up again when demand recovers. This trade-off is affected crucially by managerial expectations of firm-specific adjustment costs and, in turn, by the drivers which determine these costs. ABJ [2003, 52] identify two firm-specific characteristics which are assumed to influence the firm's level of adjustment costs, namely *asset intensity* and *employee intensity.*[13] Asset intensity is assumed to affect adjustment costs, since firm downsizes typically result in extensive write-downs of fixed assets (see, e.g., Stickney and Brown [1999, 219-222]). Employee intensity is assumed to influence adjustment costs for three reasons. Firstly, laying off redundant employees may lead to severance payments. Secondly, if demand picks up again, new employees have to be hired, which leads to recruiting costs, training costs, and a potential loss of firm-specific knowledge. Thirdly, laying off employees may induce a loss of morale and loyalty among the remaining employees, resulting in a productivity decline. ABJ [2003, 58-61] indeed find stickier costs for firms with more assets and/or employees per dollar of sales, consistent with the notion that these two measures exert a positive influence on the level of firm-specific adjustment costs. Apart from the influence of asset and employee intensity, ABJ [2003, 50 and 61] assume and find a reversal of cost stickiness, if a firm exhibits *sales decreases in two consecutive periods.* The rationale underlying this observation is the effect of a more permanent decline in demand after a second sales reduction and a potential time lag between the managerial decision to reduce redundant resources and the impact of the associated measures. Additionally, cost stickiness may be reduced by the fact that the costs of retaining idle resources might exceed the firm-specific adjustment costs after a second drop in demand (see Section 2.2.1.3).

Various follow-up studies incorporate an analysis of these determinants of firm-specific adjustment costs into their respective research design. Subramaniam and Weidenmier [2003], Diernyck and Renders [2009], Kama and Weiss [2010], He et al. [2010], Banker et al. [2011c], as well as Chen et al. [2011] provide additional empirical evidence of the effects of *asset intensity* and *consecutive sales decreases* on the intensity of cost stickiness for their respective samples. However, the results regarding the influence of *employee intensity* on the extent of cost stickiness are mixed in these studies.[14] As an example of a supporting finding of an amplifying impact of employee intensity on cost stickiness, Banker et al. [2011c, 29-30] find a significant

---

[13] These two variables are measured as the ratio of total assets to sales and as the ratio of the number of employees to sales, respectively (see ABJ [2003, 52]).

[14] The missing or inverse effect of employee intensity on cost stickiness in more recent studies, compared to ABJ (sample period 1979 to 1998), may be due to a greater proportion of *temporary* labor resulting in higher flexibility with respect to workforce adjustments and, thus, lower adjustment costs (see Chen et al. [2011, 17]). As one of many examples, Goux et al. [2001] provide empirical evidence of a far less costly adjustment of the number of fixed-term contracts (temporary workforce), compared to indefinite-term contracts.

influence of both *asset* and *employee intensity* for most countries in their sample (12 out of 17 countries in each case).

In another study, Anderson et al. [2004] confirm the impact of the firm-specific characteristics *employee intensity* and *consecutive sales decreases*, as well as of *economic growth,* on the extent of stickiness of different cost categories for a sample of service firms. However, the effect of *asset intensity* cannot be confirmed for service costs. Additionally, Anderson et al. [2004, 17] find a higher degree of service cost stickiness if *growth expectations* are high, measured ex-post by the change in sales between the current and subsequent period. The intuition underlying this relation is that the anticipated adjustment costs are higher when the probability of a near-term recovery of demand increases. Moreover, Anderson et al. [2004, 19] find a higher degree of cost stickiness for service firms in *less competitive* or *more concentrated industries*. These industries constitute an environment with fewer incentives to adapt promptly to changing conditions. Finally, Anderson et al. [2004, 19] provide empirical evidence of stickier costs of service firms that experienced higher *sales volatility* in the past, being associated with a higher probability of temporary changes in the firms' sales. Consistent with these findings, Anderson et al. [2005, 17] demonstrate a lower degree of labor cost stickiness at Southwest Airlines when *competition* increases.

Balakrishnan et al. [2004] analyze cost stickiness in US physical therapy clinics and find a significant impact of *current capacity utilization* on the extent of cost stickiness. Therapy clinics exhibit sticky cost behavior, especially if their resources are currently strained due to recent high utilization. By contrast, if clinics experience excess capacity, they show "anti-sticky" cost behavior, meaning that costs decrease more in response to falling activity than they increase when activity rises. Balakrishnan et al.'s [2004, 288] explanation of this finding is that if resources are strained, the clinic's manager is likely to make use of a decrease in activity to reduce employee overtime and compensate for a recently increased workload. Apart from that, if excess capacity exists and activity declines, the clinic's manager is likely to regard this situation as confirming a lasting reduction in demand. However, as stated above in Section 2.2.1.2, these clinic-specific results might not be transferable to manufacturing firms in all cases.

Banker et al. [2006a] confirm and extend the notion of a relationship between capacity utilization and the occurrence and extent of sticky cost behavior. They additionally analyze the impact of the direction of *previous* changes in activity on cost stickiness, instead of only considering the impact of *current* changes. According to the reasoning of ABJ, managerial expectations of future firm performance play a major role in the decision making process relating to cost adjustments. These expectations are crucially affected by the current *and* past performance of a firm. Indeed, the conclusions of ABJ apply only to years with a preceding increase in sales, whereas they are reversed if sales decrease for two consecutive years.[15] Banker et al. [2006a] attribute this occurrence of anti-sticky cost behavior in the case of two consecutive sales decreases to two causes. Firstly, managers become aware of a persisting decrease in demand, if sales decrease and have already declined in the last period. This awareness should induce managers to immediately cut redundant resources so as to adjust to the new demand level. Secondly, a previous decrease in sales should lead to surplus capacity in the current period. This inherited capacity is now available for current business activities and should therefore result in a significant decrease in current costs.

In a follow-up study, Banker et al. [2011d] use additional indicators of *managerial optimism and pessimism*, in order to provide further empirical evidence of their argument that managers' expectations decisively determine cost behavior.[16] Banker et al. [2011d, 29-31] find that the extent of cost stickiness increases if these indicators clearly and consistently signal positive prospects for the specific firm and decreases if these proxies provide conflicting or negative signals.[17] In a further study, Banker et al. [2011c, 31-32] apply the model of Banker et al. [2011d] to their international sample of Global Compustat firms and confirm the results described above for most of the analyzed countries. The countries yielding results which are not consistent with those

---

15 ABJ [2003, 60] analyze the effect of two successive decreases in sales on cost stickiness and find a mitigating influence. However, in contrast to Banker et al. [2006a], they do not analyze the effect of consecutive *increases* in sales on cost stickiness or of a sales decrease followed by an increase.

16 These additional indicators of future demand are: order backlog, macroeconomic growth, and sales forecasts by financial analysts (see Banker et al. [2011d, 11-13]).

17 Building on similar reasoning, Banker et al. [2011b] find that firms facing high demand uncertainty take measures which induce a cost structure with higher fixed costs and lower variable costs. Banker et al. [2011b, 2] argue that high demand uncertainty may result in "unusually high" demand, causing high congestion costs, due to the limited capacity of fixed inputs. In order to avoid these congestion costs, firms tend to increase the level of fixed inputs, inducing a more rigid cost structure. Although this study analyzes cost *rigidity* associated with *ex-ante* resource-adjustment decisions made by managers, in contrast to cost *stickiness* associated with *ex-post* resource-adjustment decisions, the implications of this study are also relevant for the assessment of cost stickiness (see Banker et al. [2011b, 6]). High demand uncertainty is related to a higher proportion of fixed costs, which, in turn, is related to greater total cost stickiness.

of Banker et al. [2011d] for US firms are mostly rapidly growing Asian economies, in which managerial expectations regarding future demand probably exceed the average expectations of US or European managers. Moreover, Cannon [2011, 23] finds empirical evidence that is consistent with the findings of Banker et al. [2011d] for his sample of firms in the US air transportation industry.

As stated above, sticky costs are assumed to occur due to managers leaving capacity unchanged when demand falls. However, Cannon [2011, 4] argues that costs can also be sticky in the event of *managerial capacity adjustments*. More specifically, Cannon [2011, 14-15] finds that firms in the US air transportation industry exhibit sticky cost behavior if they adjust their capacity, while the firm-specific marginal costs of adding capacity exceed the marginal benefits of removing capacity. Furthermore, Cannon [2011, 15] shows that sticky costs can occur when managers decrease output selling prices faster when demand falls than they increase selling prices when demand rises. However, the generalizability of these results appears to be uncertain, due to the industry-specific perspective, mixed results of robustness tests, and a small sample size.[18]

In addition to individual firm-specific characteristics, *interactions* between these characteristics should also have an effect on the intensity of a firm's sticky cost behavior. In this context, Calleja et al. [2006, 138] describe the effects of both previously documented (asset intensity, employee intensity) and newly introduced (debt intensity, working capital intensity) firm-specific characteristics and, especially, of interactions between these factors on the degree of cost stickiness for firms in various different countries and industries.

All in all, the impact of different determinants of firm-specific adjustment costs on cost stickiness, documented by the various studies described above, clearly confirm ABJ's explanation of a managerial trade-off between adjustment costs and idle capacity costs when demand drops.

---

[18] The sample used by Cannon [2011, 12-14] comprises only 509 total observations and only 99 observations exhibiting a decrease in sales.

2.2.3 Industry-Specific Characteristics of Cost Stickiness

As described in the preceding section, different individual characteristics determine the firm-specific resource adjustment costs and, as a consequence, firm-specific cost behavior. For the same reason, a firm's *industry affiliation* should be an important influencing factor on the occurrence and extent of cost stickiness. Firstly, documented determinants of cost stickiness, such as employee and asset intensity, should, on average, vary distinctly by industry.[19] Secondly, additional industry-specific factors, such as the intensity of competition, operational and productional environments, the average proportion of fixed and variable costs, or supply chain structures, should exert an influence on the degree of cost stickiness.[20] For instance, cost structures vary considerably between industries, reflected by a ratio of SG&A costs to sales of 5 cents per dollar of sales in the coal industry and 66 cents in the pharmaceutical product industry.[21]

Regarding the influence of industry affiliation on cost behavior, Subramaniam and Weidenmier [2003] examine the stickiness of SG&A costs separately for different industries and find the highest degree of cost stickiness for manufacturing firms, followed by service firms and merchandising firms.[22] By contrast, financial firms yield no sticky cost behavior in their sample.[23] In many accounting, and especially cost-stickiness-related research studies, financial firms (SIC codes 6000-6999) are excluded from the respective analysis due to comparability problems.[24] However, in their country-specific study, Porporato and Werbin [2010] also empirically confirm cost stickiness for a sample of South-American and Canadian banks.

---

19 Indeed, these two ratios reveal considerable variation across industries. When applying the Fama/French [1997] 49 industry definition (see Section 3.3) to an unrestricted sample of Compustat-listed US firms for the period 1990 to 2011, the asset intensity (employee intensity) yields values of 73% (29%) and 364% (92%) for the first and third quartile, respectively.

20 Numerous studies document considerable structural differences between industries (See, e.g., Ely [1991]).

21 See Section 3.3 for further details on the data sample and industry definitions.

22 Subramaniam and Weidenmier [2003, 7] classify firms into different industries by using the one-digit SIC code, resulting in the industries manufacturing (SIC codes 2 and 3), merchandising (SIC code 5), service firms (SIC codes 4, 7, and 8), and financial firms (SIC code 6).

23 In contrast to SG&A costs, Subramaniam and Weidenmier [2003, 14] obtain mixed results in a supplementary analysis of inter-industry differences in COGS stickiness.

24 See, for instance, Calleja et al. [2006, 132].

Anderson et al. [2004, 14] also confirm the impact of industry affiliation on the degree of cost stickiness by showing a varying level of cost stickiness for service firms in nine different industries.[25] According to their empirical results, the retail sector reveals almost no service cost stickiness. By contrast, the entertainment sector exhibits the highest degree of service cost stickiness. In addition, He et al. [2010, 8-10] find significant cost stickiness for Japanese merchandising, service, and especially manufacturing firms.

Not only does the degree of cost stickiness differ across industries, but established *determinants* of sticky cost behavior also exert a different influence on cost behavior in individual industries. Subramaniam and Weidenmier [2003, 16] find a significant impact of asset intensity on cost stickiness for manufacturing firms, but not for less asset-intensive industries. On the other hand, employee intensity turns out to drive COGS stickiness only in merchandising and service firms. After all, typically documented drivers of cost stickiness particularly prove to affect the degree of cost stickiness, if they are *essential* for the specific industry. In this context, Anderson et al. [2004, 17] also document a varying relevance of established drivers of cost stickiness in different industries. For instance, neither asset and employee intensity, nor sales growth prospects, affect the degree of service cost stickiness in the entertainment sector, while all three factors have a significant impact on the sticky behavior of service costs in the restaurant and hotel industry. Furthermore, as stated in Section 2.2.2, Calleja et al. [2003, 138] find different combinations of firm-specific characteristics that affect cost stickiness only in certain industries and countries.

2.2.4 Country-Specific Characteristics of Cost Stickiness

The occurrence and extent of sticky cost behavior should vary significantly *across countries* for several reasons. Firstly, firm-specific characteristics determining the individual resource adjustment costs, such as asset intensity and employee intensity may, on average, differ distinctly between countries. Secondly, countries may also exhibit different levels of optimism/pessimism concerning future economic growth, different managerial incentives affecting adjustment decisions,[26] and other differences,

[25] These industries are: entertainment, healthcare, telecommunications, transportation, wholesale, retail, restaurants and hotels, banking, and insurance.

[26] See Section 2.3 for more details on these incentives.

such as with respect to the legal system or the extent of prudential regulation. In a research study described below, Banker et al. [2011c, 38] document substantial cross-country differences in the degree of cost stickiness and find that the variation is driven by between-country differences to an average level of about 30 percent.

This notion of cross-country differences in cost stickiness is tested by Calleja et al. [2006], who analyze sticky cost behavior for a sample of US, UK, German, and French firms. Calleja et al. [2006, 133] find a considerably higher level of cost stickiness for French and German firms, compared to US and UK firms, and attribute this finding to differing systems of corporate governance affecting managerial cost behavior. In *common law countries*, such as the USA and the UK, firms focus primarily on shareholder value maximization and hence emphasize reporting more timely accounting data (Calleja et al. [2006, 129]).[27] In *code-law countries*, such as France and Germany, on the other hand, firms aim to reconcile the interests of various groups of stakeholders, such as banks, unions, and the workforce. These differences result in varying levels and drivers of adjustment costs determining the average country-specific extent of cost stickiness.

Banker and Chen [2006a] also examine cross-country differences in cost stickiness for an even more comprehensive sample of 19 OECD countries.[28] After controlling for established drivers of cost stickiness at the firm level, Banker and Chen [2006a, 25] find a significantly varying extent of cost stickiness across firms in different countries. They attribute this variance to different macro-level labor market characteristics. In their analysis, Banker and Chen [2006a, 26] empirically document a higher degree of cost stickiness when the bargaining power of unions is high, which potentially complicates employee layoffs. However, this impact of bargaining power is mitigated if unions are more centralized and coordinated in the bargaining process. Furthermore, sticky cost behavior tends to be stronger in countries with a low level of unemployment insurance benefits and also in those with strict employment protection legislation. All in all, this study underlines that cost reactions to changes in activity are not only influenced by firm-specific factors, but also by economy-wide conditions.

---

[27] The estimation results for US firms are comparable to those found by Subramaniam and Weidenmier, [2003] who also examine the stickiness of *operating costs* for US firms (see Section 2.2.1.1).

[28] These countries are: Australia, Austria, Belgium, Canada, Denmark, Finland, France, Germany, Ireland, Italy, Japan, the Netherlands, Norway, Portugal, Spain, Sweden, Switzerland, the United Kingdom and the USA.

In a follow-up study, Banker et al. [2011a] use cross-country variation in the strictness of the employment protection legislation in 19 OECD countries, as a proxy for labor adjustment costs, in order to further substantiate the varying influence of country-specific adjustment costs on the extent of sticky cost behavior.[29] As expected, Banker et al. [2011a, 23] find a higher degree of average country-specific cost stickiness in countries with strict employment protection legislation. In a further follow-up study mentioned at the beginning of this subsection, Banker et al. [2011c] again conduct a comprehensive analysis of cost stickiness in 19 different countries included in the Global Compustat database. These range from low-income developing countries (e.g., Indonesia, India) to high-income developed countries (e.g., Sweden, Switzerland).[30] Banker et al. [2011c, 28] find strong evidence of cost stickiness for nearly all of these countries and additionally, consistent with the results in Banker and Chen [2006a], significant variation in the average country-specific extent of sticky cost behavior.

In a research study focusing on cost behavior in a single country other than the USA, De Medeiros and De Souza Costa [2004] analyze the sticky behavior of costs in Brazil, the world's seventh largest economy, and find a significantly higher degree of cost stickiness relative to the results for US firms presented by ABJ. De Medeiros and De Souza Costa [2004, 12] explain this result in terms of a greater reluctance of Brazilian managers to lay off employees, due to a lower level of social security relative to the USA, a lower proportion of skilled Brazilian employees, and the development status of Brazil as an emerging economy in general.[31]

In their analysis of a differences-in-costs-model (see Section 2.4), Argilés and García-Blandón [2009] not only focus on a specific country, namely Spain, but also on

[29] More specifically, Banker et al. [2011a, 17] use an employment protection legislation index, which comprises 14 items, such as the country-specific average length of the notice period before dismissal, or the country-specific average level of severance pay. This index shows substantial cross-country variation with scores from 0.2 for the USA and 4.3 for Portugal, on a scale from zero to six.

[30] Despite the identical number of 19 different countries, these countries differ to a large degree from the economies analyzed by Banker and Chen [2006a]. The countries considered by Banker et al. [2011c] are: Australia, Brazil, Canada, China, France, Germany, Hong Kong, Indonesia, India, Japan, Korea, Malaysia, Singapore, South Africa, Sweden, Switzerland, Taiwan, Thailand, the United Kingdom, and the USA.

[31] As a further example of a cost stickiness study focusing on a specific emerging economy, Özkaya and Yükcü [2011] re-estimate ABJ's model for a sample of non-financial Turkish firms and empirically confirm the occurrence of cost stickiness and the results of all supplementary analyses conducted by ABJ for Turkey.

a specific industry that is exposed to constant change, namely farms. Despite the fact that farms operate under very specific conditions, such as a crucial dependence on climatic conditions, Argilés and García-Blandón [2009, 18] find cost stickiness for all analyzed agricultural cost categories. In a further country-specific study, Diernyck and Renders [2009] document the stickiness of labor costs for a sample of Belgian private companies, thus taking advantage of transparent disclosure of different components of labor costs in this country. Moreover, Poporato and Werbin [2010] provide empirical evidence of cost stickiness in the banking sector in Argentina, Brazil, and Canada.

In further single-country studies, He et al. [2010] and Kajiwara and Yasukata [2011] find significant SG&A cost stickiness for Japanese companies, and thus additionally support the generalizability of the findings of previous studies analyzing the cost stickiness of US firms only. While different Japan-specific factors potentially result in either *lower* cost stickiness (e.g., fewer agency problems and more intensive monitoring of managers than in US firms) or *greater* stickiness (e.g., long-term focus of firms, employee layoffs more unusual), the extent of SG&A cost stickiness is relatively comparable to the level documented for US firms. Taken together, cost stickiness proves to be a world-wide cost phenomenon, whose intensity depends partly on individual country-specific conditions.

2.3 Cost Stickiness and Managerial Incentives

The majority of cost-stickiness-related research studies focus exclusively on factors influencing the level of adjustment costs. As the second main cause of sticky cost behavior, ABJ [2003, 49-50] identify decisions made by self-interested managers to maximize personal utility, instead of contributing to the objectives of the firm's shareholders. Typical examples are managerial hesitance to accept a loss of status, revise overambitious past investment decisions, or layoff longstanding employees. A few more recent studies take a closer look at these managerial incentives as important drivers of sticky cost behavior.

In one of these recent studies, Chen et al. [2011, 18-20] find that managerial empire building incentives are positively related to the extent of cost stickiness.[32] This

[32] In this study, managers' empire building incentives are measured by free cash flow, CEO horizon, CEO tenure, and compensation structure.

finding supports the notion that self-interested managers play an important role in the emergence of sticky cost behavior. Moreover, Chen et al. [2011, 21-22] find that corporate governance measures, which are designed to prevent conflicts of interest, can be used to mitigate the amplifying effect of empire building incentives on cost stickiness.[33] Supplementary analyses also show that these incentives exert a stronger influence on cost stickiness in mature firms and in those for which SG&A investments tend to create low future value.[34] Banker et al. [2011c, 34] re-estimate the model of Chen et al. [2011] for their sample of Global Compustat firms. The effect of higher free cash flows, as a proxy for stronger empire-building incentives, predominantly yields the expected algebraic sign, but is statistically significant only for seven of 18 analyzed countries. Thus, international evidence to support the conclusions of Chen et al. [2011] turns out to be mixed.

Dierynck and Renders [2009] also conduct an analysis of the influence of managerial incentives on cost asymmetry. They examine the relation between the stickiness of labor costs and earnings management incentives for a sample of Belgian firms. Dierynck and Renders [2009, 23] find that earnings management incentives cause a more symmetric firm-specific cost pattern. They attribute this finding to managerial actions to avoid losses in firms reporting relatively small positive earnings or small increases in earnings. However, the level of cost stickiness is again higher, if earnings management is implemented through accrual manipulations, instead of real earnings management.

A significant influence of managerial incentives on cost stickiness is also documented empirically by Wiersma [2010], who analyzes the impact of managerial reward systems on the stickiness of costs. Wiersma [2010, 18] finds that a relatively higher level of short-term-oriented bonuses is associated with greater incentives to decrease a firm's resource level immediately after a decrease in sales, that is, with lower cost stickiness. On the other hand, a lower proportion of short-term bonuses

---

33 The quality of firm-specific corporate governance is determined by the variables board size, percentage of independent directors, CEO/chairman separation (both proxies for board independence), institutional shareholders, an anti-takeover index, and staggered board (both proxies for anti-takeover provisions).

34 See Chen et al. [2011, 23-26].

motivates managers to delay resource adjustments and to temporarily bear the costs of idle capacity, due to the possibility that sales rebound in the near future.[35]

In order to analyze the impact of managerial incentives on cost stickiness from a broader perspective, Kama and Weiss [2010] distinguish between two potential drivers of sticky costs, namely current deliberate resource adjustments made by self-interested managers to meet short-term earnings targets, and constraints determined by past technology choices made to maximize firm value. In line with the studies mentioned above, Kama and Weiss [2010, 18] find that incentives to avoid losses or earnings decreases significantly diminish cost stickiness, because these incentives induce managers to cut resources faster and to a greater extent. Furthermore, consistent with Banker et al. [2006a], Kama and Weiss [2010, 19] provide evidence of a positive impact of constraints set by past technology decisions on the degree of cost stickiness, as for instance, by investments in production facilities and human resourses.[36] These constraints determine the future ability of the firm to respond to changes in the activity level, meaning that more flexible resources, associated with lower adjustment costs, result in a lower degree of cost stickiness. By combining these two sources of sticky cost behavior, Kama and Weiss [2010, 20] demonstrate an interdependency between the two effects, while indicating a dominating effect of incentive considerations over technological constraints. According to the empirical results, cost stickiness caused by pre-determined technological constraints is overcompensated in the presence of managerial incentives to meet earnings targets.

Banker et al. [2011c] re-estimate the model of Kama and Weiss [2010] for their sample of Global Compustat firms, confirming the results described above for at least some of the analyzed countries. The impact of incentives to avoid earnings decreases is statistically significant for seven of 19 countries, whereas the impact of incentives to

---

[35] In their research study on the relationship between cost behavior and executive compensation, Caylor and Lopez [2010] find that cost behavior explains the previously documented finding of a weak link between executive compensation and earnings underperformance Although this study does not test directly for the effects of cost stickiness, it gives additional insight into the potential for compensation committees to mitigate sticky cost behavior by means of an improved design of executive bonus compensation.

[36] Kama and Weiss [2010, 12] utilize demand uncertainty, measured by revenue volatility known in prior periods, as a proxy for past technology decisions made to meet higher future demand uncertainty.

avoid losses is significant for eight countries.[37] In a further study, Banker et al. [2011d] extend the model introduced by Kama and Weiss [2010] to a two-period model and argue that firms which are supposed to avoid losses are, to a large extent, actually those which experienced a previous decline in sales. Banker et al. [2011d, 34-36] suggest that this interdependency can only be revealed by a multi-period model.

In contrast to the studies presented above, Balakrishnan et al. [2011] provide empirical evidence of a more limited impact of short-term managerial behavior on the sticky behavior of costs than suggested by prior literature. Balakrishnan et al. [2011] show that past decisions on cost structure decisively determine the extent of costs which are controllable in the short run and thus constrain the influence of short-term managerial incentives on cost stickiness.[38] On the other hand, Wiersma [2010, 17-19] finds a significant influence of managerial incentives, proxied by the managerial reward structure, on cost stickiness, even after controlling for the firm-specific cost structure. Apparently, both the determinants of adjustment costs and of managerial incentives, cause sticky cost behavior. However, the relative importance of these two causes appears to represent an open research question.

2.4 Criticism of the Cost Stickiness Concept

Although the methodology and findings presented by ABJ have been widely accepted in the accounting research literature and extended by various follow-up studies, the established approach of measuring cost stickiness, as well as the assumed underlying causes, have also been challenged in recent research. In their comprehensive study on cross-country differences in cost stickiness, Banker et al. [2011c] directly address two of the major studies which challenge the empirical validity of previous findings on sticky costs. Banker et al. [2011c, 40] claim that, after correcting for different econometric issues and sample selection criteria, these two studies "actually lend additional support to the sticky costs findings." For each of these

[37] Remarkably, Banker et al. [2011c, 33] find no empirical evidence of an effect of incentives to avoid losses on the level cost stickiness for US data. This clearly contradicts Kama and Weiss [2010]. The authors explain this result by the use of a more recent sample than that of Kama and Weiss [2010]. This sample contains more observations from after the Enron scandal and the Sarbanes-Oxley act in 2001 and 2002, respectively. Measures taken in response to these events tend to impede earnings management practices in the subsequent years, potentially affecting the estimation results.

[38] See Section 2.4 for more details on this study.

two studies (Anderson and Lanen [2009] and Balakrishnan et al. [2011]), both respective points of views are described below.

In a frequently cited study, Anderson and Lanen [2009] criticize ABJ for interpreting the asymmetric reaction of costs to increases and decreases in sales as evidence of active cost management, in contrast to a "mechanically" cost response. Anderson and Lanen [2009, 3] argue that a mechanical model of cost changes without managerial intervention represents an inadequate benchmark, since all cost realizations are considered necessarily to be the result of managerial decisions made at some point in time. Apart from criticizing the underlying reasoning, Anderson and Lanen [2009] also raise two major objections to the sample selection and methodology used by ABJ. Firstly, Anderson and Lanen [2009, 25] find no significant stickiness of discretionary cost categories other than SG&A costs, such as advertising costs, and the non-financial measure number of employees. Secondly, Anderson and Lanen [2009, 9] argue that including "unusual" firm-year observations for which sales and costs move in opposite directions, that is, increasing sales accompanied by a cost decrease and decreasing sales accompanied by a cost increase, is not consistent with the theory established by ABJ. Rather, these observations should indicate fundamental changes in the firm's environment. Indeed, Anderson and Lanen [2009, 28] find much weaker empirical evidence of sticky cost behavior, when they exclude these "unusual" observations from their analysis. This finding suggests that that these observations influence the empirical estimations fundamentally.

Banker et al. [2011c] directly address the two objections raised by Anderson and Lanen [2009]. Regarding the first objection of a lack of stickiness of different cost categories, Banker et al. [2011c, 24 and 56] reply that the sticky cost theory does not imply that all cost categories are necessarily sticky at all times, particularly if they are associated with low or no adjustment costs, such as those of advertising. Furthermore, Banker et al. [2011c, 56-57] find significant stickiness of the non-financial measure number of employees in the event of a prior sales increase, and significant anti-stickiness in the case of a prior sales decrease, when using the refined cost stickiness model of Banker et al. [2011d], which considers managerial optimism and pessimism.[39] Regarding the second objection with respect to the inclusion of "unusual" observations for which sales and costs change in different directions,

[39] The approach of this study is presented in Section 2.2.3.

Banker et al. [2011c, 24 and 57-61] argue that these observations are not necessarily "unusual". They could, for instance, be caused rather by convex adjustment costs for which gradual resource adjustments are meaningful. Under the condition that the "unusual" observations indeed reflect factors that are unrelated to deliberate cost management, Banker et al. [2011c, 58] argue that Anderson and Lanen's [2009] approach of simply eliminating these observations is tainted with a crucial selection bias. The rationale underlying this argument is the fact that other "unusual" observations, such as much higher increases in costs than increases in sales and much higher decreases in costs than decreases in sales, are in turn not eliminated. According to simulation analyses by Banker et al. [2011c], this selection bias amplifies the influence of the latter group of "unusual" observations and thus leads to distortions in the model estimation, causing an empirical result of a lack of stickiness for costs that are in fact sticky.

As stated above, the model specification used to measure and detect cost stickiness, as well as the prevailing explanation in terms of short-run managerial decisions, is also criticized by Balakrishnan et al. [2011]. Building on Balakrishnan et al. [2004] and Kama and Weiss [2011], Balakrishnan et al. [2011] point out that past cost structure decisions fundamentally affect the measurement of cost stickiness and therefore constitute an important omitted variable in previous studies using the established model by ABJ. According to Balakrishnan et al.'s [2011] reasoning and simulation analyses, fixed cost effects inherited from past cost structure decisions potentially bias regression coefficients in this model.[40] Moreover, they argue that the log-specification of the established model causes distortions, since it assumes a stationary elasticity, whereas systematic shifts in the distribution of the elasticity appear to be likely.[41] When applying an alternative percent-specification model that controls for both these effects, cost stickiness weakens for the entire cross-sectional sample of firms and even vanishes altogether for various subsamples. Banker et al. [2011d, 38-39] address the argument of Balakrishnan et al. [2011] that a more refined model is necessary to analyze the sticky behavior of costs and argue that their two-

[40] In their country and industry-specific analysis, Porporato and Werbin [2010] provide empirical evidence of cost stickiness even when controlling for cost structure. Thus, despite the limited sample of their study, the relevance of significant distortions caused by an omitted variable bias in previous studies appears to be questionable.

[41] The elasticity in this model is the percentage change in SG&A costs between two periods, given a one percent change in sales within the same time frame. Balakrishnan et al. [2011] assume that this elasticity is not constant, but depends on the growth rate of sales.

period model which incorporates proxies for managerial optimism fulfills this requirement.[42]

As with the response to the above criticism expressed by Anderson and Lanen [2009], Banker et al. [2011c] also address the objections raised by Balakrishnan et al. [2011]. Banker et al. [2011c, 25 and 62-76] argue that the simulation results of Balakrishnan et al. [2011] are driven by a crucial assumption, which is inconsistent with patterns of actual data. More precisely, Banker et al. [2011c, 66] show that Balakrishnan et al. [2011] assume a positive relationship between the firm-specific sales in the previous period and the firm's probability of achieving sales increases in the current period; that is, larger firms are assumed to be more likely to grow than smaller ones. This assumption is clearly inconsistent with Compustat data from the last few decades. Banker et al. [2011c] provide empirical evidence of cost stickiness when this assumption is removed, even after controlling for cost structure effects. Furthermore, Banker et al. [2011c] argue that the estimation results of the alternative percent-specification model suggested by Balakrishnan et al. [2011] actually indicate distinctly significant cost stickiness, if the sample selection criteria are corrected for a severe sample selection bias. More precisely, Banker et al. [2011c, 71] point out that Balakrishnan et al. [2011] reasonably exclude observations for which SG&A costs exceed sales in the current year, but do not exclude observations for which SG&A costs are greater than sales in the *previous* year. Since the model consists of variables which measure the differences in sales and costs between the current and previous period, this partial exclusion of distorting observations causes a severe downward bias in the estimated coefficients. For a "corrected" sample, Banker et al. [2011c, 72] obtain coefficient estimates from Balakrishnan et al.'s [2011] alternative model which provide clear empirical evidence of cost stickiness.

A third study also criticizes the methodology applied by ABJ and various subsequent studies. Argilés and García-Blandón [2009] point out that in the well-established line of research on *price* stickiness, a differences-in-prices model is commonly used instead of the log-linear model specification introduced by ABJ. Argilés and García-Blandón [2009, 582] criticize ABJ for not justifying their approach adequately and for not testing alternative models sufficiently. They further argue that a log-linear model constitutes an inadequate approach for analyzing samples formed by

42 See Section 2.2.3 for more details on this study.

very homogeneous firms, as is the case for their sample of Spanish agricultural firms. Argilés and García-Blandón [2009, 581] assume that missing evidence of sticky cost behavior in different sub-samples documented by prior studies can be attributed to model misspecifications with respect to relatively homogeneous sample units.

All in all, a few research studies raise reasonable objections to the findings and methodology presented by ABJ. However, Banker et al. [2011c] address most of these objections in a detailed and comprehensible manner, thus validating their theory underlying sticky cost behavior.

2.5 Applications of the Cost Stickiness Concept to Related Financial Research

The observation of an asymmetric cost response to decreases and increases in activity fundamentally affects various concepts of financial and management accounting, which implicitly assume or even explicitly require a proportional reaction of costs to activity changes. However, only a small number of studies have applied the methods and implications of the research on cost stickiness to related research areas. Regarding the interdependency of management and financial accounting topics, Weiss [2010, 1467] points out that "although such a multi-disciplinary approach has not been common in prior literature, (...) combining the perspectives of management and financial accounting can be fruitful." Similarly, Banker et al. [2011c, 14] highlight that "(...) most of the empirical literature on sticky costs focus on characterizing various aspects of sticky cost behavior. However, much less attention has been paid to the important implications of sticky costs for other areas."

As a notable exception, Banker and Chen [2006b] apply the cost stickiness concept to fundamental analysis. They find that an earnings prediction model which explicitly incorporates cost variability and cost stickiness outperforms two alternative established prediction models in forecasting one-year-ahead returns on equity. These two alternative models do not consider cost variability and cost stickiness, but rather disaggregate earnings into operating and non-operating income components (Fairfield et al. [1996]), and into cash flow and accrual components (Sloan [1996]), respectively. In a subsequent study, Banker et al. [2011b, 31-34] further enhance this model by incorporating additional proxies for managerial optimism and pessimism, resulting in an even greater predictive power of the model.[43]

In another application of the cost stickiness concept, Homburg and Nasev [2008] analyze the impact of cost stickiness on conditional conservatism, that is, on a timelier and more sensitive earnings response to bad news than to good news.[44] Homburg and Nasev [2008] introduce an interpretation of managers' decisions to bear the costs of redundant resources as a "risky project" and find that cost stickiness increases the asymmetric timeliness of earnings. More specifically, Homburg and Nasev [2008, 20] empirically document a diminishing effect of cost stickiness on the timeliness of earnings for good-news firms and an intensifying effect for bad-news firms. Furthermore, Homburg and Nasev [2008, 20-21] suggest that conditional conservatism assists the market in distinguishing between *efficient* sticky costs firms, for which sales recover shortly after a demand drop, and *inefficient* sticky costs firms, for which sales decline permanently. As an extension to the interpretation of cost stickiness as an investment in a risky project, Karatzias [2009] examines the impact of cost stickiness on future performance and whether this relation is determined by the firm-specific investment-opportunities set.[45] Following Homburg and Nasev [2008], Karatzias [2009, 2] distinguishes between efficient firms which made the right choice to bear the costs of unused resources and inefficient firms which kept resources for unproductive reasons, such as the personal considerations of self-interested managers. However, Karatzias [2009, 37-38 and 42] arrives at mixed results.[46] Consequently, he considers the contribution of his study as a motivation for future research on performance prediction.

Anderson et al. [2007] conduct another application of the cost stickiness concept to fundamental analysis. Building on their finding that SG&A costs are sticky, Anderson et al. [2007] argue that the impact of an increase in the ratio of SG&A costs to sales on future earnings is determined by the direction of the simultaneous change in sales. The results, conclusions, and limitations of this study are presented in more

---

43 See Section 2.2.2 for a more detailed description of the study and the applied proxies.

44 For more details on the concept of conditional conservatism, see Basu [1997].

45 Karatzias [2009, 22] measures the investment-opportunity set of a firm by the market-to-book assets ratio.

46 The models used by Karatzias [2009, 37] "explain only a very small amount of the variance" in future performance and the firm-specific investment opportunities moderate the impact of cost stickiness in only one of several analyzed cases.

detail in Chapter 3 of this doctoral thesis, together with an alternative approach to analyzing the information content of the SG&A ratio.

A further study which combines cost stickiness with a financial accounting research topic is Weiss' [2010] analysis of the impact of cost stickiness on the accuracy of financial analysts' earnings forecasts. Weiss [2010, 1458-1462] constructs a variable that measures the degree of cost stickiness for a given firm in a given quarter and shows that firms with stickier cost behavior have less accurate quarterly consensus earnings forecasts than firms with less sticky cost behavior.[47] In addition, Weiss [2010, 1462-1465] finds that firms with stickier costs exhibit lower analyst coverage and that the earnings surprises of these firms cause a weaker market reaction. In his study, Weiss [2010, 1444 and 1462] assumes that "analysts recognize cost behavior to a reasonable extent." In a comprehensive analysis presented in Chapter 4 of this doctoral thesis, I address the research question of whether analysts recognize cost behavior and show that the answer to this question depends crucially on the forecast horizon. As explained in detail in this chapter, late forecasts, that is, those issued shortly before the announcement date, do consider cost stickiness, whereas early forecasts, that is, those issued well before the announcement date, disregard cost stickiness.

All in all, only a small number of studies combine the established cost stickiness theory with related financial research areas. The following Chapters 3 and 4 of this doctoral thesis address this research gap by presenting cost stickiness-related implications for two important fields of firm performance prediction, namely fundamental analysis and analysts' forecasts.

---

[47] Most prior research studies on the sticky behavior of costs use a regression analysis of panel data to provide general empirical evidence of the emergence of cost stickiness or to show the influence of specific factors on its extent. Weiss [2011] introduces a new cost stickiness measure at the firm level, in order to distinguish between firms with sticky and anti-sticky cost behavior. Although this firm-specific measure also exhibits some limitations, such as a loss of many firm-year-observations due to the requirement of both an increase and a decrease in the respective firm's sales during the last four quarters, it offers a wide range of opportunities for analyzing the impact of various factors separately for sticky and anti-sticky firm. This opportunity has not yet been seized by subsequent research studies on the consequences of sticky cost behavior.

3 Cost Stickiness and the Information Content of the SG&A Ratio

The following chapter addresses the relationship between cost stickiness and fundamental analysis by using the example of contradictory interpretations of an increase in the ratio of selling, general, and administrative costs to sales (SG&A ratio). Anderson et al. [2007] attribute the existence of positive and negative impacts of an increase in this important ratio on future performance to the sticky behavior of costs. I provide an alternative approach to determine the information content of the SG&A ratio and compare this approach to the method suggested by Anderson et al. [2007]. The analysis in the following chapter is largely based on my research study, which I have presented at the *2009 AAA Northeast Region Meeting* in Cambridge, Massachusetts and at the *Journal of Management Accounting Research Conference* in Seattle, Washington. A former version of this study has also been published as a double-peer-reviewed journal article in the 2010 issue of the *Journal of Management Accounting Research.*[48]

3.1 Introduction

According to the prevalent interpretation in management accounting textbooks,[49] an increase in the ratio of selling, general, and administrative costs to sales (SG&A ratio) is associated with inefficient cost management and *negative* impacts on future performance. This argument is reasonable if SG&A costs escalate beyond managerial control and consequently increase unintentionally. Apart from this, a few studies in the recent research literature have analyzed characteristics of SG&A costs that allow for a *positive* influence of a rising SG&A ratio on future profitability. This contrary reasoning is based primarily on the potential creation of intangible assets through SG&A expenditures (Banker et al. [2006b, 2011e]) and the retention of SG&A resources during a current demand drop in anticipation of a forthcoming recovery of sales, referred to as "cost stickiness" (Anderson et al. [2007]).

---

[48] See Baumgarten et al. [2010].

[49] See, for instance, Bernstein and Wild [1998, 583].

My empirical results reflect these opposing effects of an increasing SG&A ratio, since I find no significant impact of changes in the SG&A ratio on subsequent earnings changes, based on my entire sample. A more differentiated approach appears to be essential, in order to deduce earnings-relevant information from the SG&A ratio. I argue that the crucial point is a distinction between whether the increase in the SG&A ratio is *intended* by management to enhance profitability or merely reflects costs getting out of hand. This distinction should capture both existing interpretations which allow for a positive effect of an increasing SG&A ratio, namely the creation of intangible assets and the deliberate retention of resources, as they both imply intention.

In order to determine whether the SG&A ratio is raised intentionally, I use past efficiency in SG&A cost management. Only if management has the expertise to consistently keep SG&A costs under control, a deliberate application of SG&A resources appears to be feasible. In order to decide whether a company is able to control its SG&A costs, I compare its SG&A ratio to the respective industry mean. Accordingly, I consider an increase in the SG&A ratio to be intended if a company has a previous SG&A ratio *below* the industry average, as this constitutes an indicator of effective SG&A cost control. These intended increases are supposed to have the objective of exerting a positive impact on future profitability. Indeed, I find a significantly positive influence of an increasing SG&A ratio on future operating earnings for SG&A cost-efficient companies. For companies exhibiting difficulties in SG&A cost management in the past, I find a significantly negative impact on future operating earnings, consistent with the traditional interpretation of cost inefficiency.

Furthermore, I reveal the origin of the aggregated effect on future operating earnings by decomposing the SG&A ratio's impact into the influences on future sales, cost of goods sold, and SG&A costs. To the best of my knowledge, my study is the first to decompose the effect of changes in the SG&A ratio in this manner. By means of my approach, I show that increases in the SG&A ratio by SG&A cost-efficient firms significantly decrease the future cost of goods sold. This result supports the notion of SG&A expenses functioning partly as deliberate investments in improving operational processes. Examples could be enhancements of IT systems, re-organizations of operational procedures, investments into R&D, and expansions of supporting departments such as in-house consulting. A second differentiation of my sample by past efficiency in the management of the cost of goods sold confirms the evidence of such deliberate investments. The positive impact of intended SG&A

expenses is especially distinct for firms with considerable latitude for reducing the cost of goods sold.

As briefly outlined in Section 2.5, Anderson et al. [2007] also differentiate between two types of changes in the SG&A ratio. They build on the concept of cost stickiness, distinguishing between periods of falling and rising sales, and find that SG&A ratio increases have a positive impact on future earnings in periods of falling sales. I conduct a direct empirical comparison of this approach and my differentiation by SG&A cost efficiency. This comparison reveals a more significant, stronger, and more persistent signaling effect in the case of the segmentation by cost efficiency. In addition, my approach has explanatory power that is incremental to the differentiation by the direction of sales changes. The positive impact of an increasing SG&A ratio on future profitability is especially strong if a firm simultaneously exhibits falling sales and SG&A cost efficiency.

My findings are important for various users of financial statements. External analysts and capital market investors attach great importance to the SG&A ratio, since SG&A costs form a high share of sales revenue (Lazere [1996, 28]), on average, 32 percent in my sample. My conclusions can support them in correctly interpreting this important ratio. In addition, my results have significant implications for management accounting, in particular. I present evidence that targeted SG&A investments can help to reduce manufacturing costs, resulting in higher future operating earnings. An awareness of this interdependency between SG&A expenses and the cost of goods sold could assist managers in determining the optimal balance between these two types of cost.

The remainder of this chapter is structured as follows. Section 3.2 discusses my study in the context of prior research on the SG&A ratio in fundamental analysis. Section 3.3 introduces the empirical models I use in my analysis and describes sample statistics. Section 3.4 presents and discusses the empirical results. In Section 3.5, I distinguish my approach from the cost stickiness explanation. In Section 3.6, I conduct several robustness tests. Section 3.7 summarizes the results and presents conclusions for the interpretation of changes in the SG&A ratio.

3.2 The SG&A Ratio in Fundamental Analysis

Previous studies dealing with the information content of the SG&A ratio arrive at contradictory conclusions. Lev and Thiagarajan [1993] estimate the incremental value-relevance of several signals in fundamental analysis, including the SG&A ratio. For most of the years that they investigate, a rising SG&A ratio exhibits a *negative* effect on subsequent returns. Additionally, their study reveals a more intense returns-fundamentals relation under certain macroeconomic circumstances, thus highlighting the relevance of a contextual fundamental analysis. Abarbanell and Bushee [1997] analyze whether current changes in fundamental signals yield useful information about subsequent earnings changes. In an unconditioned sample, the SG&A ratio is not significantly related to one-year-ahead earnings changes. By contrast, it exhibits a negative impact if earnings declined in the previous year, as well as during low-GDP periods.

Banker et al. [2006b] provide evidence of a possible *positive* effect of an increase in the SG&A ratio. They find indications of a positive impact on future operating income caused by current SG&A expenditure and explain this result in terms of a potential creation of intangible assets. Banker et al. [2011e] also refer to a positive impact of SG&A investments in their analysis of the relationship between equity incentives and SG&A expenditure.

A further explanation of a positive impact of an increasing SG&A ratio on future earnings is based on SG&A cost stickiness. As described in detail in Chapter 2, ABJ introduce this term by empirically documenting that SG&A costs tend to decrease less with falling sales than they increase in times of rising sales. Important for the interpretation of increases in the SG&A ratio, ABJ attribute cost stickiness to managers adjusting resources due to their expectations of future demand. According to this argument, managers will prefer to delay resource reductions in times of falling sales if they anticipate a forthcoming recovery of demand. Given such a temporary demand shock, the adjustment costs of reducing resources and ramping them up again shortly afterwards should exceed the costs of surplus capacity.

Building on their finding of cost stickiness, Anderson et al. [2007] extend the earnings prediction model of Abarbanell and Bushee [1997] that was described above. Deviating from this study, Anderson et al. [2007] focus on the SG&A ratio and differentiate between companies with rising and falling sales. They find a positive relation between changes in the SG&A ratio and subsequent earnings during periods with declining sales, explained by the deliberate retention of resources as a result of optimistic managerial expectations.

The conflicting interpretations of the impact of an increase in the SG&A ratio highlight the relevance of my analysis. I aim to reconcile these contradictory findings and argue that it is decisive to distinguish between rises in the SG&A ratio that occur deliberately, and those that reflect costs escalating out of control. Intended increases should exert a positive impact on future profitability, thus reflecting effective investments. Additionally, I contribute to the existing literature by decomposing the aggregated impact of SG&A ratio changes on future earnings components.

3.3 Research Design and Data

3.3.1 Research Design

3.3.1.1 Impact on Future Operating Earnings per Share

I estimate a modified replication of an established forecast model originally designed by Lev and Thiagarajan [1993] for the prediction of returns and later adopted by Abarbanell and Bushee [1997], as well as by Anderson et al. [2007] to forecast earnings. My model relates changes in subsequent operating earnings per share to changes in the current SG&A ratio, current changes in operating earnings per share, and further fundamental ratios as control variables.[50] I analyze changes in *operating* earnings per share, since Compustat's operating earnings solely comprise sales, cost of goods sold, and SG&A costs. I decompose the impact of the SG&A ratio on future operating earnings into the influences on these three particular components in the next subsection. Moreover, non-operating earnings components are removed, so as to focus on the part of income that is generated by the company's core activity. Excluding one-time effects as special items or other nonrecurring earnings components yields forecasting improvements (Fairfield et al. [1996, 354]).[51]

---

[50] Ou [1990, 161] emphasizes that financial ratios provide predictive information on future earnings changes beyond the individual announcement effect of the current earnings change itself.

[51] An analysis of the impact on future earnings per share instead of future *operating* earnings per share leads to similar conclusions, as presented in Section 3.6.

I implement two different variables for changes in the SG&A ratio, so as to facilitate a contextual analysis.[52] This approach is similar to that of Anderson et al. [2007], who distinguish between periods of rising or falling sales. By contrast, I aim to differentiate between whether or not an increase in the SG&A ratio is intended to enhance future profitability.[53] I include one variable $SG\&A^{sga\_low}$ for increases that are assumed to be intended to improve future profitability and one variable $SG\&A^{sga\_high}$ for changes in the SG&A ratio that are assumed to reflect costs getting out of control. Both interpretations of a positive effect of an increasing SG&A ratio, the creation of intangible assets and the deliberate retention of resources, imply intention. Accordingly, filtering for intended increases in the SG&A ratio should fully reveal their positive impacts. I utilize the past relation between the individual SG&A ratio and its industry mean as a proxy for the quality of the company's SG&A cost management and thus for the ability to prudently increase the SG&A ratio on purpose. Consequently, I assume that a company deliberately adjusts its SG&A costs in the event of a past SG&A ratio below the industry average. If the ratio was above the industry average in the previous period, I assume deficiencies in SG&A cost control and conclude that increases in the SG&A ratio of these companies should mainly be not intended. I apply the Fama/French [1997] 49 industry definition to calculate the industry average of the SG&A ratio.[54] By using *industry* averages as a benchmark, I consider differences in the SG&A ratio that are due to industry-specific characteristics. Indeed, the average ratio of SG&A costs to sales differs considerably between the 49 industry categories, showing values between 5 cents (coal industry) and 66 cents (pharmaceutical products industry) per dollar of sales revenue. Moreover, the mean standard deviation of the SG&A ratio *within* the industry classes (25 cents) is significantly lower than in the entire sample (35 cents). Consequently, my approach should allow a differentiation between SG&A cost-efficient and inefficient companies

---

52 For instance, Sloan [2001, 191] points out the improvement of fundamental analysis models by the introduction of explanatory variables that are tailored to the particular context.

53 I also vary the framework used in Anderson et al. [2007] by introducing two dummy variables in addition to the existing set of control variables. If a criterion such as SG&A cost efficiency or the direction of sales changes is assumed to affect the influence of the SG&A signal on subsequent earnings, this criterion can also influence future earnings itself. I control for this direct effect by including two dummy variables for the direction of current sales changes and for SG&A cost efficiency. Indeed, both dummies significantly influence future earnings. Nevertheless, I arrive at the same conclusions without these dummy variables, so that comparability with the results in Anderson et al. [2007] is ensured.

54 I arrive at the same conclusions when applying the two-digit SIC, three-digit SIC, and four-digit SIC industry classification schemes, instead of the Fama/French 49 industry definition.

which considers industry specifics to a large extent. My regression equation is the following:

$$COEPS1_{i,t+1} = \alpha + \beta_1 \, SG\&A_{i,t}^{sga\_low} + \beta_2 \, SG\&A_{i,t}^{sga\_high} + \delta \, COEPS_{i,t} + \sum_{j=1}^{12} \gamma_j \, Other\ Signals_{i,j,t} + \varepsilon_{i,t+1} \qquad [3.1]$$

where

$$COEPS1_{i,t+1} = \frac{Operating\ Earnings\ per\ Share_{i,t+1} - Operating\ Earnings\ per\ Share_{i,t}}{P_{i,t-1}}$$

$SG\&A_{i,t}^{sga\_low} = \frac{SG\&A_{i,t}}{Sales_{i,t}} - \frac{SG\&A_{i,t-1}}{Sales_{i,t-1}}$ if the firm-specific SG&A ratio was below or equal to the industry average in the previous period or 0 otherwise;

$SG\&A_{i,t}^{sga\_high} = \frac{SG\&A_{i,t}}{Sales_{i,t}} - \frac{SG\&A_{i,t-1}}{Sales_{i,t-1}}$ if the firm-specific SG&A ratio was above the industry average in the previous period or 0 otherwise;

$$COEPS_{i,t} = \frac{Operating\ Earnings\ per\ Share_{i,t} - Operating\ Earnings\ per\ Share_{i,t-1}}{P_{i,t-1}}$$

while using selling, general, and administrative expenses (Compustat data item #189, mnemonic *xsga*) for $SG\&A_{i,t}$ and net sales (#12, mnemonic *sale*) for $Sales_{i,t}$. In order to compute *COEPS* and *COEPS1*, I use operating income before depreciation (#13, mnemonic *oibdp*) divided by common shares used to calculate earnings per share (#54, mnemonic *cshpri*) for $Operating\ Earnings\ per\ Share_{i,t}$ and the stock price at fiscal year end (#199, mnemonic *prcc*) for $P_{i,t-1}$. The control variables are described in detail in the empirical results section in Table 3.2.

3.3.1.2 Impact on Future Sales, Cost of Goods Sold, and SG&A Costs

Operating earnings can be calculated roughly by subtracting the cost of goods sold and SG&A costs from sales revenue:

$$Operating\ Earnings = Sales - COGS - SG\&A$$

I use this decomposition to analyze the impact of current changes in the SG&A ratio on subsequent changes in sales, cost of goods sold, and SG&A costs. By means of this approach, I aim to identify the source of influence on future changes in operating earnings. Thus, I introduce three variations of forecast model [3.1] by exchanging the dependent variable:

$$\frac{Sales_{i,t+1} - Sales_{i,t}}{Marketcap_{i,t-1}} = \alpha + \beta_1\, SG\&A_{i,t}^{sga\_low} + \beta_2\, SG\&A_{i,t}^{sga\_high} + \delta\, COEPS_{i,t} + \sum_{j=1}^{12} \gamma_j\, Other\ Signals_{i,j,t} + \varepsilon_{i,t+1} \qquad [3.2]$$

$$\frac{COGS_{i,t+1} - COGS_{i,t}}{Marketcap_{i,t-1}} = \alpha + \beta_1\, SG\&A_{i,t}^{sga\_low} + \beta_2\, SG\&A_{i,t}^{sga\_high} + \delta\, COEPS_{i,t} + \sum_{j=1}^{12} \gamma_j\, Other\ Signals_{i,j,t} + \varepsilon_{i,t+1} \qquad [3.3]$$

$$\frac{SG\&A_{i,t+1} - SG\&A_{i,t}}{Marketcap_{i,t-1}} = \alpha + \beta_1\, SG\&A_{i,t}^{sga\_low} + \beta_2\, SG\&A_{i,t}^{sga\_high} + \delta\, COEPS_{i,t} + \sum_{j=1}^{12} \gamma_j\, Other\ Signals_{i,j,t} + \varepsilon_{i,t+1} \qquad [3.4]$$

I use the cost of goods sold (Compustat data item #41, mnemonic *cogs*) for $COGS_{i,t}$, as well as monthly common shares outstanding (*CSHOQ*) multiplied by monthly price close (*PRCCM*) from the Center for Research in Security Prices (CRSP) to calculate the market capitalization. $Marketcap_{i,t-1}$ is the average market capitalization of firm *i* during year *t*-1. The other variables are calculated as described above.

3.3.1.3 Influence of Potential for Enhancements of Operating Processes

I moreover examine whether the current level of efficiency in operational processes has an influence on the effect of an increasing SG&A ratio. I assume that a positive impact of intended changes in the SG&A ratio will be stronger if the current potential for cost reduction in the operating business is high. For this reason, I apply the ratio of cost of goods sold to sales (COGS ratio) as an indicator of operating efficiency. Consequently, I partition the sample a second time, now additionally taking into account the past relationship of the COGS ratio to its industry mean.[55] All in all, I obtain four different SG&A ratio signals in the earnings forecast model:

$$
\begin{aligned}
COEPS1_{i,t+1} = \alpha + \beta_1\, SG\&A_{i,t}^{sga\_low\_cogs\_low} + \beta_2\, SG\&A_{i,t}^{sga\_low\_cogs\_high} \\
+ \beta_3\, SG\&A_{i,t}^{sga\_high\_cogs\_low} + \beta_4\, SG\&A_{i,t}^{sga\_high\_cogs\_high} \\
+ \delta\, COEPS_{i,t} + \sum_{j=1}^{12} \gamma_j\, Other\ Signals_{i,j,t} + \varepsilon_{i,t+1}
\end{aligned}
\qquad [3.5]
$$

where

$SG\&A_{i,t}^{sga\_low\_cogs\_low} = \frac{SG\&A_{i,t}}{Sales_{i,t}} - \frac{SG\&A_{i,t-1}}{Sales_{i,t-1}}$ if the firm-specific SG&A ratio *and* the firm-specific COGS ratio were below or equal to their industry averages in the previous period or 0 otherwise;

$SG\&A_{i,t}^{sga\_low\_cogs\_high} = \frac{SG\&A_{i,t}}{Sales_{i,t}} - \frac{SG\&A_{i,t-1}}{Sales_{i,t-1}}$ if the firm-specific SG&A ratio was below or equal to its industry average and the firm-specific COGS ratio was above its industry average in the previous period or 0 otherwise;

$SG\&A_{i,t}^{sga\_high\_cogs\_low} = \frac{SG\&A_{i,t}}{Sales_{i,t}} - \frac{SG\&A_{i,t-1}}{Sales_{i,t-1}}$ if the firm-specific SG&A ratio was above its industry average and the firm-specific COGS ratio was below or equal to its industry average in the previous period or 0 otherwise;

$SG\&A_{i,t}^{sga\_high\_cogs\_high} = \frac{SG\&A_{i,t}}{Sales_{i,t}} - \frac{SG\&A_{i,t-1}}{Sales_{i,t-1}}$ if the firm-specific SG&A ratio *and* the firm-specific COGS ratio were above their industry averages in the previous period or 0 otherwise;

and the other variables as described above.

---

[55] I again apply the Fama/French [1997] 49 industry definition, in order to determine the industry averages of the COGS ratio.

3.3.2 Sample Data

I utilize Compustat and CRSP data provided by Wharton Research Data Services (WRDS) including active and inactive US firms for the time period 1980 to 2006. In most regressions, the sample ranges from 1984 to 2005, due to the need for previous periods in order to compute some of the control variables, as well as one subsequent period for one-year-ahead changes in the dependent variables. To avoid distortions caused by outliers, I trim the data by deleting observations of each variable in the top and bottom 0.5 percent of its distribution (Chen and Dixon [1972]),[56] as well as observations with missing values for any of the variables. Furthermore, I remove firm-year observations that can be assigned to the financial services industries.[57] The final basic sample contains 5,524 firms with 26,102 firm-year observations.

Table 3.1: Descriptive Statistics on the SG&A Ratio

Panel A: Descriptive Statistics on Past SG&A Efficiency

	SG&A Ratio Below Industry Mean		SG&A Ratio Above Industry Mean	
Year	Proportion	Mean SG&A Ratio	Proportion	Mean SG&A Ratio
1984	61%	16.3%	39%	37.6%
1985	63%	18.0%	37%	39.4%
1986	63%	19.3%	37%	42.6%
1987	63%	19.3%	37%	42.3%
1988	64%	19.2%	36%	42.7%
1989	64%	19.9%	36%	43.9%
1990	63%	19.3%	37%	43.1%
1991	62%	19.5%	38%	42.5%
1992	61%	19.5%	39%	40.6%
1993	63%	19.0%	37%	42.5%
1994	61%	17.9%	39%	39.4%
1995	62%	18.2%	38%	41.4%
1996	63%	18.3%	37%	44.3%
1997	64%	20.4%	36%	49.8%

[56] In addition to this trimming, I conduct a supplementary analysis, considering only the middle 90 percent in the distribution of SG&A cost efficiency within each industry. I come to similar estimation results and identical conclusions despite the sample limitation. Obviously, outliers do not bias my estimation results.

[57] When I repeat all regressions including the financial services industries, I arrive at the same conclusions.

Table 3.1 (continued)

1998	67%	22.3%	33%	57.7%
1999	65%	21.3%	35%	62.2%
2000	68%	24.0%	32%	57.3%
2001	67%	27.0%	33%	71.7%
2002	71%	28.7%	29%	82.4%
2003	69%	25.9%	31%	72.2%
2004	71%	25.1%	29%	71.8%
2005	76%	27.1%	24%	79.4%
Average all Periods	65%	21.4%	35%	50.9%

Panel B: Descriptive Statistics on Past SG&A and Cost-of-Goods-Sold Efficiency

	SG&A Ratio Below Industry Mean		SG&A Ratio Above Industry Mean	
Criterion in *t*-1	**COGS Ratio Below Industry Mean**	**COGS Ratio Above Industry Mean**	**COGS Ratio Below Industry Mean**	**COGS Ratio Above Industry Mean**
Proportion	22%	43%	27%	8%
Mean Sales	1,321	1,561	758	419
Mean Operating Earnings	291	181	102	35
Mean SG&A Ratio	28%	18%	48%	57%
Mean COGS Ratio	50%	75%	49%	70%

Table 3.1 provides descriptive statistics on the segmentation of the sample by past cost efficiency in the SG&A ratio and in the relation of the cost of goods sold to sales (COGS ratio). The basic sample includes 5,524 U.S. firms with 26,102 firm-year observations. A company is assigned to the respective "below industry mean" category if the firm-specific ratio was below or equal to the average of its industry in the previous period. On the other hand, an assignment to the "above industry mean" category occurs in the case of an individual ratio above the industry average. For the classification of industries, I utilize the Fama/French [1997] 49 industry definition excluding the financial services industry classes 45 to 48 (obtainable from: http://mba.tuck.dartmouth.edu/pages/faculty/ken.french/).

Panel A shows the proportions resulting from the differentiation by past SG&A cost efficiency, as well as the mean SG&A ratio values of both groups for the years of my observation period.

Panel B presents descriptive statistics on the segmentation of the sample by past SG&A *and* COGS efficiency. Mean sales and operating earnings are stated in millions of dollars.

3.3.3 Descriptive Statistics

Descriptive statistics concerning the SG&A ratio and the differentiation of the sample by the past SG&A and COGS ratios are presented in Table 3.1.

As illustrated in Panel A of Table 3.1, the separation according to the relationship between a company's SG&A ratio and the mean of its own industry leads to an average segmentation of about 65 percent of companies below and 35 percent above the individual industry average. A closer look at the year-by-year statistics reveals that the proportion of companies below the industry mean varies between 61 and 76 percent during the observation period, showing moderately higher shares in recent years. The SG&A ratio of the group above the industry mean exhibits, on average, a clearly higher SG&A ratio value of 50.9 percent, compared to a mean of 21.4 percent in the below-average class, suggesting that the segmentation by past SG&A cost efficiency is a distinct differentiation criterion. Furthermore, SG&A cost efficiency turns out to be a persistent characteristic. On average, only about nine percent of the observed firms switch groups between two periods.[58]

Panel B of Table 3.1 provides descriptive statistics for the dual differentiation by past SG&A cost efficiency *and* past efficiency in the cost of goods sold. On average, only 22 percent of the companies are efficient in both cost categories. These firms earn higher operating earnings combined with lower sales than those companies that are efficient in the management of SG&A costs and inefficient with regard to the cost of goods sold. I expand on the four groups in the following subchapter that presents the empirical results of the dual differentiation.

---

[58] Additional descriptive statistics reveal that both groups exhibit remarkably similar values in terms of sales growth and leverage. In contrast, firms that are SG&A cost-efficient exhibit higher total assets and returns on assets and equity. In order to rule out the possibility that I am capturing effects due to different levels of firm size or profitability, I recalculated my regression model including different additional variables controlling for these characteristics. These modifications do not change my results notably.

3.4 Results

3.4.1 Impact on Future Operating Earnings per Share

The estimation results of my earnings forecast model are presented in Table 3.2. In their analysis of the information content of the SG&A ratio, Anderson et al. [2007] run year-by-year regressions and report aggregated Fama-MacBeth [1973] coefficient and standard error estimates. The Fama-MacBeth [1973] approach avoids correlation in the residuals across different firms within the same year, but does not consider dependence of the residuals across years for a given firm (Petersen [2009, 436]). In this context, Gow et al. [2010, 508] point out that accounting research models, such as the earnings prediction model used by Anderson et al. [2007] and by my study, are particularly affected by both cross-sectional and time-series dependence. Gow et al. [2010, 509] further argue that it is necessary to properly adjust for both forms of dependency, so as to avoid producing miss-specified test statistics and spurious inferences. In order to control for dependencies across years *and* firms, I run OLS regressions for all my analyses, while computing standard errors clustered by time and firms, as suggested by Petersen [2009, 453]. Additionally, I estimate aggregated Fama-MacBeth [1973] estimates, so as to ensure the comparability of my results with those of Anderson et al. [2007]. Apart from an insignificant influence of increase in the SG&A ratio by SG&A cost-inefficient firms, the Fama-MacBeth [1973] estimates yield similar regression coefficients and t-values, resulting in almost identical conclusions.

I also tested the model for potential heteroscedasticity by performing White's [1980] test. The hypothesis of heteroscedasticity was rejected at the 1 percent level for all regressions in this chapter. In addition, I tested each of the following regressions for multicollinearity by computing variance inflation factors (vif). The values for all variables are close to 1, well below common cutoffs.

As expected, the coefficient of the SG&A ratio signal in the case of a SG&A ratio below the industry average in the last period (β_1) exhibits a significantly positive value of 0.157. The coefficient is highly significantly positive with a *t*-statistic of 4.13. This result supports my assumption that increases in the SG&A ratio by SG&A cost-efficient firms positively influence future profitability. In this context, I consider the existence of SG&A cost efficiency as an indicator of intended SG&A spending. An additional regression analysis also confirms this significantly positive influence in the second year after the initial increase in the SG&A ratio. This persistence of the positive impact underpins my assumption and furthermore indicates the sustainability of the intended investments.

The SG&A ratio signal coefficient of the companies that were allocated to the class of companies with a past SG&A ratio above the industry average (β_2) shows a significantly negative coefficient of -0.019 (*t*-statistic: -2.28). This result is consistent with the prevalent expectation of a negative influence of an increasing SG&A ratio when costs are getting out of hand.

Regarding the control variables, all variables featuring a significant coefficient, except for the earnings quality and audit qualification signals, exhibit the expected algebraic signs. In particular, the dummy variables for sales increases and SG&A efficiency, the inventory, capital expenditures, and tax signals significantly influence future operating earnings changes.[59] In the following subsection, I extend my analysis in order to elaborate on the interactions underlying the impact of the SG&A ratio on future operating earnings.

---

[59] Note that some of the control variables, such as the tax signal, naturally exhibit lower explanatory power than in comparable analyses (e.g., Abarbanell and Bushee [1997]), since I analyze the influence on changes in *operating* earnings per share, in order to ensure consistency with the results of the subsequent disaggregation into the effects on future changes in sales, SG&A costs, and COGS. See Section 3.6 for the estimation results of an alternative regression on changes in future full earnings per share.

Table 3.2: Analysis of Changes in Future Operating Earnings

$$COEPS1_{i,t+1} = \alpha + \beta_1\, SG\&A^{sga\_low}_{i,t} + \beta_2\, SG\&A^{sga\_high}_{i,t} + \delta\, COEPS_{i,t} + \sum_{j=1}^{12} \gamma_j\, Other\ Signals_{i,j,t} + \varepsilon_{i,t+1}$$

$$SG\&A\ Signal_{i,t} = \frac{SG\&A_{i,t}}{Sales_{i,t}} - \frac{SG\&A_{i,t-1}}{Sales_{i,t-1}}$$

Coefficient	INT	SG&A sga_low	SG&A sga_high	COEPS	$D^{saleincr}$	D^{sga_low}	INV	AR	CAPX	GM	ETR	EQ	AQ	LF	LEV	Growth
					Other Signals											
Value	0.027	0.157	-0.019	-0.028	-0.024	-0.013	-0.175	0.043	-0.004	0.081	-0.053	0.012	0.049	0.001	0.001	0.001
t-statistic	5.76	4.13	-2.28	-1.35	-4.08	-2.34	-5.14	1.58	-2.76	1.47	-1.83	3.80	2.01	0.09	0.72	0.34
adjusted R^2	4.5%															

Table 3.2 shows the estimation results of a regression model forecasting one-year-ahead changes in operating earnings per share. The sample includes 5,524 US firms with 26,102 firm-year observations from 1984 to 2005. I run OLS regressions while computing standard errors clustered by time and firms, as suggested by Petersen [2009, 453]. In order to facilitate comparability of the results, this table is designed in the style of Anderson et al. [2007]. The variables are in detail:

$$COEPS1_{i,t+1} = \frac{Operating\ Earnings\ per\ Share\ (\text{Compustat data item \#13/\#54})_{i,t+1} - Operating\ Earnings\ per\ Share_{i,t}}{P(\#199)_{i,t-1}}$$

$$SG\&A^{sga\_low}_{i,t} = \frac{SG\&A(\#189)_{i,t}}{Sales(\#12)_{i,t}} - \frac{SG\&A_{i,t-1}}{Sales_{i,t-1}}$$ if the firm-specific SG&A ratio was below or equal to the industry-average in the previous period or 0 otherwise

$$SG\&A^{sga\_high}_{i,t} = \frac{SG\&A_{i,t}}{Sales_{i,t}} - \frac{SG\&A_{i,t-1}}{Sales_{i,t-1}}$$ if the firm-specific SG&A ratio was above the industry-average in the previous period or 0 otherwise

$$COEPS_{i,t} = \frac{Operating\ Earnings\ per\ Share_{i,t} - Operating\ Earnings\ per\ Share_{i,t-1}}{P_{i,t-1}}$$

Table 3.2 (continued)

Control variables:

Direction of changes in sales $(D_{i,t}^{saleincr}) = 1$ for increasing sales between period t - 1 and t, 0 otherwise

SG&A efficiency $(D_{i,t}^{sga\_low}) = 1$ if the firm-specific SG&A ratio was below or equal to the industry-average in period t - 1, 0 otherwise

$$\text{Inventory } (INV_{i,t}) = \frac{Inventory(\#3)_{i,t}}{Sales_{i,t}} - \frac{Inventory_{i,t-1}}{Sales_{i,t-1}}$$

$$\text{Accounts Receivable } (AR_{i,t}) = \frac{Accounts\ Receivable(\#2)_{i,t}}{Sales_{i,t}} - \frac{Accounts\ Receivable_{i,t-1}}{Sales_{i,t-1}}$$

$$\text{Capital Expenditure } (CAPX_{i,t}) = \frac{Firm\ Capital\ Expenditure\ (\#30)_{i,t}}{Industry\ Capital\ Expenditure_{i,t}} - \frac{Firm\ Capital\ Expenditure_{i,t-1}}{Industry\ Capital\ Expenditure_{i,t-1}}$$

$$\text{Gross Margin } (GM_{i,t}) = \frac{Gross\ Margin\ (\#12\text{-}\#41)_{i,t-1}}{Sales_{i,t-1}} - \frac{Gross\ Margin_{i,t}}{Sales_{i,t}}$$

$$\text{Effective Tax Rate } (ETR_{i,t}) = \left[\left(\frac{1}{3}\sum_{\tau=1}^{3} Tax\ Rate_{i,t-\tau}\right) - Tax\ Rate_{i,t}\right] \cdot COEPS_{i,t}$$

$$\text{where } Tax\ Rate_{i,t} = \frac{Tax\ Expense\ (\#16)_{i,t}}{EBT\ (\#170 + \#65)_{i,t}}$$

Earnings Quality $(EQ_{i,t}) = 0$ for LIFO, 1 for FIFO or other (#59)

Audit Qualification $(AQ_{i,t}) = 0$ for Unqualified, 1 for Qualified or other (#149)

$$\text{Labor Force } (LF_{i,t}) = \frac{\dfrac{Sales_{i,t-1}}{Employees(\#29)_{i,t-1}} - \dfrac{Sales_{i,t}}{Employees_{i,t}}}{\dfrac{Sales_{i,t-1}}{Employees_{i,t-1}}}$$

$$\text{Leverage } (LEV_{i,t}) = \frac{Long\text{-}term\ Debt\ (\#9)_{i,t}}{Equity\ (\#60)_{i,t}} - \frac{Long\text{-}term\ Debt_{i,t-1}}{Equity_{i,t-1}}$$

$$\text{Sales Growth } (Growth_{i,t}) = \frac{Sales_{i,t}}{Sales_{i,t-1}} - \frac{Sales_{i,t-1}}{Sales_{i,t-2}}$$

Variables $INV_{i,t}$ to $Growth_{i,t}$ are defined according to Abarbanell and Bushee [1997] and Anderson et al. [2007].

3.4.2 Impact on Future Sales, Cost of Goods Sold, and SG&A Costs

In order to examine the influence of the SG&A ratio on subsequent operating earnings in more detail, I analyze the effect of SG&A ratio changes on future sales, cost of goods sold, and SG&A costs. To the best of my knowledge, mine is the first study to conduct such an in-depth analysis of the influence of changes in the SG&A ratio on individual income statement elements. I fill this gap by re-executing regression [3.1], but now applying future changes in sales, cost of goods sold, or SG&A costs as dependant variable. I present the results of these regressions in Table 3.3.

Changes in the SG&A ratios of both SG&A cost-efficient and inefficient firms do not significantly influence the following period's *changes in sales*, depicted in Panel A of Table 3.3. Consequently, the positive impact on subsequent operating earnings in the case of SG&A cost-efficient firms is not attributed to a future boost in sales in response to investments into SG&A resources. Rather, the positive influence corresponds to the significantly negative influence of SG&A ratio increases by SG&A cost-efficient firms on the future *cost of goods sold*, presented in Panel B of Table 3.3. By contrast, such a significantly negative influence is not given for firms that are unable to manage their SG&A costs efficiently.

In the regression on subsequent changes in *SG&A costs*, the coefficient of the current SG&A ratio signal features an insignificant value for SG&A cost-efficient firms, as shown in Panel C of Table 3.3. Hence, the increase in subsequent operating earnings in the case of these firms does not result from lower future SG&A costs. This outcome indicates that increases in the SG&A ratio by SG&A cost-efficient firms are not temporary or the result of cyclical shifts. Instead, they appear to be intended, because future SG&A costs do not decrease significantly in response to a current increase in the SG&A ratio. In contrast, a current increase in the SG&A ratio by firms showing SG&A cost inefficiency leads to a significant decrease in future SG&A costs. This finding supports my assumption that increases in the SG&A ratio by these firms are mainly beyond managerial control, reflecting unintended fluctuations.

All in all, the positive influence of an increase in the SG&A ratio on subsequent operating earnings for SG&A cost-efficient firms is attributed to a significantly negative impact on the future cost of goods sold. This negative effect indicates that SG&A expenditures of SG&A cost-efficient firms partially represent deliberate investments in operating efficiency. This assumption is supported by my additional finding that increases in the SG&A ratio by SG&A cost-efficient firms enhance the future gross margin that functions as a "measure of manufacturing efficiency" in financial analysis (Atkinson et al. [2007, 616]). When I replace the dependant variable of regression [3.1] by changes in the future gross margin, I obtain a significantly positive coefficient for SG&A cost-efficient companies. Again, this relationship is absent in the case of companies that are SG&A cost-inefficient. Therefore, the positive impact on future operating earnings appears to result from targeted investments in process optimization. For instance, these targeted SG&A investments could be used to enhance the contribution of supporting departments and IT systems, to advance human resource development, boost R&D activities, and slim down the production process. Spence [1984, 101] expresses this strategy as follows: "Firms compete over time by expending resources with the purpose of reducing their costs."

Such investments in operational efficiency will not be equally successful for every firm. Success should rather depend on the current individual level of operational efficiency. For this reason, I hereafter refine my analysis to consider the present degree of cost efficiency in operational processes.

Table 3.3: Impact on Future Sales, Cost of Goods Sold, and SG&A Costs

Panel A: One-Year-Ahead Changes in Sales

$$\frac{Sales_{i,t+1} - Sales_{i,t}}{Marketcap_{i,t-1}} = \alpha + \beta_1 \, SG\&A_{i,t}^{sga\_low} + \beta_2 \, SG\&A_{i,t}^{sga\_high} + \delta \, COEPS_{i,t} + \sum_{j=1}^{12} \gamma_j \, Other\ Signals_{i,j,t} + \varepsilon_{i,t+1}$$

Variable	Coefficient	t-value	Mean adj. R²
$SG\&A^{sga\_low}$	-0.136	-1.24	8.2%
$SG\&A^{sga\_high}$	-0.013	-0.43	

Panel B: One-Year-Ahead Changes in the Cost of Goods Sold

$$\frac{COGS_{i,t+1} - COGS_{i,t}}{Marketcap_{i,t-1}} = \alpha + \beta_1 \, SG\&A_{i,t}^{sga\_low} + \beta_2 \, SG\&A_{i,t}^{sga\_high} + \delta \, COEPS_{i,t} + \sum_{j=1}^{12} \gamma_j \, Other\ Signals_{i,j,t} + \varepsilon_{i,t+1}$$

Variable	Coefficient	t-value	Mean adj. R²
$SG\&A^{sga\_low}$	-0.204	-2.16	8.1%
$SG\&A^{sga\_high}$	-0.011	-0.51	

Panel C: One-Year-Ahead Changes in SG&A Costs

$$\frac{SG\&A_{i,t+1} - SG\&A_{i,t}}{Marketcap_{i,t-1}} = \alpha + \beta_1 \, SG\&A_{i,t}^{sga\_low} + \beta_2 \, SG\&A_{i,t}^{sga\_high} + \delta \, COEPS_{i,t} + \sum_{j=1}^{12} \gamma_j \, Other\ Signals_{i,j,t} + \varepsilon_{i,t+1}$$

Variable	Coefficient	t-value	Mean adj. R²
$SG\&A^{sga\_low}$	-0.027	-1.07	9.9%
$SG\&A^{sga\_high}$	-0.013	-4.54	

Table 3.3 presents the estimation results of OLS regressions with standard errors clustered by time and firms on one-year-ahead changes in sales (Panel A), cost of goods sold (Panel B), and SG&A costs (Panel C). I use monthly common shares outstanding (*CSHOQ*) multiplied by monthly price close (*PRCCM*) from CRSP to calculate a firm's market capitalization. $Marketcap_{i,t-1}$ is the mean market capitalization of firm *i* during year *t*-1. The sample, variables, and procedures are depicted in Table 3.2.

3.4.3 Influence of Potential for Enhancements of Operating Processes

The extent of feasible reductions in the cost of goods sold by SG&A investments should depend on both the ability to adequately adjust SG&A expenses and the current degree of room for improvement in the production process. If a firm's operational efficiency is already high, further improvement will be difficult. If, however, the firm has not yet attained operational efficiency, there is still potential for improvement by means of targeted SG&A investments. To test this, I introduce a second differentiation of the SG&A ratio signal. As before, I consider the ability to maintain the previous SG&A ratio within reasonable limits as an indicator of intentional SG&A expenditure. In addition, I separate firms by the previous relationship between their ratio of cost of goods sold to sales and the industry mean by proxy for room for improvement in operational productivity. Thus, I obtain four variables for changes in the SG&A ratio that belong to different subsamples. Figure 3.1 illustrates the classification into the four subcategories.

Figure 3.1: Benchmarking Approach

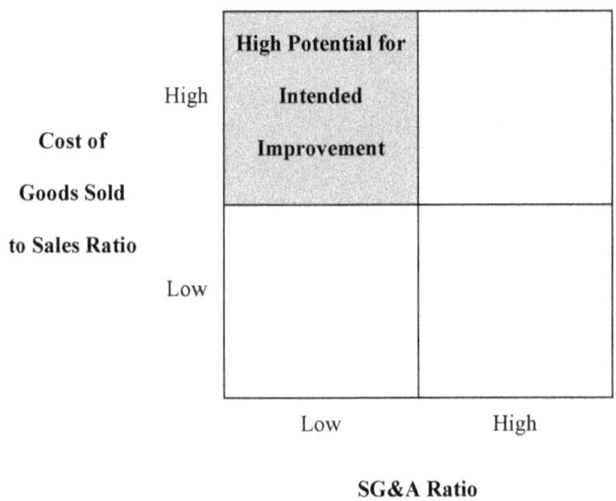

Firms in the left column exhibit a below-average SG&A ratio. They should be able to adjust their SG&A resources intentionally, in order to increase future profitability. Firms in the upper left corner additionally have an above-average ratio of cost of goods sold to sales, thus exhibiting ample latitude for an improvement in operational processes. For this subgroup, I expect the highest positive impact of SG&A investments on future profitability. The results in Table 3.4 confirm this assumption.

Table 3.4: Analysis of Changes in Future Operating Earnings Considering the Potential for Improvement in Operational Processes

$$COEPS1_{i,t+1} = \alpha + \beta_1\, SG\&A_{i,t}^{sga\_low\_cogs\_low} + \beta_2\, SG\&A_{i,t}^{sga\_low\_cogs\_high} + \beta_3\, SG\&A_{i,t}^{sga\_high\_cogs\_low} + \beta_4\, SG\&A_{i,t}^{sga\_high\_cogs\_high} + \delta\, COEPS_{i,t} + \sum_{j=1}^{12} \gamma_j\, Other\ Signals_{i,j,t} + \varepsilon_{i,t+1}$$

	$SG\&A^{sga\ low\ cogs\ low}$	$SG\&A^{sga\ low\ cogs\ high}$	$SG\&A^{sga\ high\ cogs\ low}$	$SG\&A^{sga\ high\ cogs\ high}$
Coefficient	0.088	0.277	-0.019	-0.018
t-value	2.69	3.97	-1.42	-2.06

Table 3.4 shows the estimation results of a regression on one-year-ahead changes in operating earnings per share. The sample, variables, and procedures are depicted in Table 3.2, except for the definition of the SG&A ratio signal. In this analysis, the SG&A ratio signal is differentiated by past cost efficiency in the SG&A ratio *and* in the ratio of cost of goods sold to sales. The four SG&A ratio signals are defined as:

$SG\&A_{i,t}^{sga\_low\_cogs\_low} = \frac{SG\&A_{i,t}}{Sales_{i,t}} - \frac{SG\&A_{i,t-1}}{Sales_{i,t-1}}$ if the firm-specific SG&A ratio *and* the firm-specific COGS ratio were below or equal to their industry averages in the previous period or 0 otherwise;

$SG\&A_{i,t}^{sga\_low\_cogs\_high} = \frac{SG\&A_{i,t}}{Sales_{i,t}} - \frac{SG\&A_{i,t-1}}{Sales_{i,t-1}}$ if the firm-specific SG&A ratio was below or equal to its industry average and the firm-specific COGS ratio was above its industry average in the previous period or 0 otherwise;

$SG\&A_{i,t}^{sga\_high\_cogs\_low} = \frac{SG\&A_{i,t}}{Sales_{i,t}} - \frac{SG\&A_{i,t-1}}{Sales_{i,t-1}}$ if the firm-specific SG&A ratio was above its industry average and the firm-specific COGS ratio was below or equal to its industry average in the previous period or 0 otherwise;

$SG\&A_{i,t}^{sga\_high\_cogs\_high} = \frac{SG\&A_{i,t}}{Sales_{i,t}} - \frac{SG\&A_{i,t-1}}{Sales_{i,t-1}}$ if the firm-specific SG&A ratio *and* the firm-specific COGS ratio were above their industry averages in the previous period or 0 otherwise.

The impact of the SG&A ratio signal on one-year-ahead changes in operating earnings is actually considerably higher for companies simultaneously featuring SG&A cost efficiency and a COGS ratio above the industry mean. For these companies, the SG&A ratio coefficient (β_2) amounts to 0.277, compared to the value for the companies exhibiting efficiency with regard to both cost types (β_1) of 0.088.[60] In contrast, both classes with an above-average SG&A ratio yield negative coefficients. Accordingly, SG&A expenses do not exert a positive impact on future

60 The two coefficients are significantly different at the 1 percent level.

earnings if they are not raised intentionally, even if there is still room for improvement in operational efficiency.[61]

Recall that from the descriptive statistics in Panel B of Table 3.1, companies which are efficient both in SG&A costs and in the cost of goods sold achieve higher operating earnings, but lower sales than firms that are only efficient in managing their SG&A costs. Furthermore, the latter group exhibits a moderately lower SG&A ratio of 18 percent and simultaneously a notably higher Cogs ratio of 75 percent. This implies that companies which are cost-efficient overall have already achieved an optimal balance of SG&A costs and the cost of goods sold. Consequently, firms in the SG&A efficient/Cogs inefficient category may deliberately accept moderate increases in the SG&A ratio, so as to obtain higher reductions in the cost of goods sold and thus rising operating earnings. These firms might have been too restrained with respect to nonmanufacturing costs and costs of supporting departments. This underinvestment may have caused inefficiency and obsolete structures in manufacturing processes, leading to the higher cost of goods sold. Accordingly, an increase in the SG&A ratio may be positive, particularly if it is intended *and* there is still sufficient potential for improving the manufacturing processes.

My results indicate the benefits of benchmarking in terms of cost efficiency. By comparing their efficiency in SG&A costs and the cost of goods sold with their competitors, managers can classify their firms into one of the four groups illustrated in Figure 3.1. This classification can support them in evaluating to what extent possible investments in operational processes by means of SG&A expenses might be promising.

[61] In a supplementary analysis of the impact on the future gross margin, I confirm the stronger positive effect of SG&A investments by companies exhibiting a combination of SG&A cost efficiency and existing potential for operational improvements. Only these companies show a statistically significant SG&A ratio coefficient regarding the future gross margin, as an approved indicator of both productivity and profitability.

3.5 Differentiation from an Explanation in Terms of Cost Stickiness

Based on the concept of cost stickiness, Anderson et al. [2007] distinguish between SG&A ratio changes in periods of rising and falling sales. They find a positive impact of SG&A ratio increases on future earnings for firms with declining sales and attribute this impact to the deliberate retention of surplus SG&A resources when managers anticipate an upcoming sales recovery. In the following, I compare the approach of Anderson et al. [2007] with my own segmentation. I find that my approach creates a clearer signal of positive SG&A effects and provides explanatory power which is incremental to the differentiation in terms of rising and falling sales.

First, I execute two regressions using identical data samples, one on the basis of my differentiation by cost efficiency (henceforth "cost efficiency model") and one based on the direction of changes in sales (henceforth "stickiness model"). A comparison of the estimation results shows that the SG&A ratio signal coefficient in the cost efficiency model (0.157) is significantly higher than the coefficient in the stickiness model (0.028), as presented in Panel A of Table 3.5. The positive effect on future operating earnings in the cost efficiency model is not only stronger, but also more persistent than that in the stickiness model. The positive impact of SG&A ratio increases by SG&A cost-efficient firms persists in the year after next with a coefficient of 0.141 (*t*-statistic: 2.83) when regressing on operating earnings changes two years later. As shown in Panel B of Table 3.5, there is no such *continuous* effect in the stickiness model. The coefficient of the SG&A ratio signal for firms with falling sales loses significance in the year after next (*t*-statistic: 1.43).

I furthermore find no empirical evidence of the reasoning behind the explanation by cost stickiness. According to this reasoning, an increasing SG&A ratio in periods of falling sales should indicate the manager's expectation of a forthcoming sales recovery. On the contrary, I do not find a positive impact of SG&A ratio changes on future sales in periods of falling sales, neither when I analyze the impact on sales in the following year, nor in the year after next.

Table 3.5: Comparison of the Differentiation Criteria

Panel A: Direct Comparison of the Effects on One-Year-Ahead Changes in Operating Earnings

Model 1: Separation by Cost Efficiency ("Cost Efficiency Model")

$$COEPS1_{i,t+1} = \alpha + \beta_1\, SG\&A_{i,t}^{sga\_low} + \beta_2\, SG\&A_{i,t}^{sga\_high} + \delta\, COEPS_{i,t} + \sum_{j=1}^{12} \gamma_j\, Other\ Signals_{i,j,t} + \varepsilon_{i,t+1}$$

Model 2: Separation by the Direction of Changes in Sales ("Stickiness Model")

$$COEPS1_{i,t+1} = \alpha + \beta_1\, SG\&A_{i,t}^{sales\_fall} + \beta_2\, SG\&A_{i,t}^{sales\_rise} + \delta\, COEPS_{i,t} + \sum_{j=1}^{12} \gamma_j\, Other\ Signals_{i,j,t} + \varepsilon_{i,t+1}$$

Category	Coefficient	t-value	Mean adj. R^2
$SG\&A^{sga\_low}$	0.157	4.13	4.5%
$SG\&A^{sales\_fall}$	0.028	2.61	4.4%
difference	0.129	2.12	

Panel B: Effects on Operating Earnings in the Period after Next

Model 1: Separation by Cost Efficiency ("Cost Efficiency Model")

$$COEPS1_{i,t+2} = \alpha + \beta_1\, SG\&A_{i,t}^{sga\_low} + \beta_2\, SG\&A_{i,t}^{sga\_high} + \delta\, COEPS_{i,t} + \sum_{j=1}^{12} \gamma_j\, Other\ Signals_{i,j,t} + \varepsilon_{i,t+2}$$

Model 2: Separation by the Direction of Changes in Sales ("Stickiness Model")

$$COEPS1_{i,t+2} = \alpha + \beta_1\, SG\&A_{i,t}^{sales\_fall} + \beta_2\, SG\&A_{i,t}^{sales\_rise} + \delta\, COEPS_{i,t} + \sum_{j=1}^{12} \gamma_j\, Other\ Signals_{i,j,t} + \varepsilon_{i,t+2}$$

Category	Coefficient	t-value	Mean adj. R^2
$SG\&A^{sga\_low}$	0.141	2.83	4.2%
$SG\&A^{sales\_fall}$	0.042	1.43	4.2%

Panel C: Analysis of the Incremental Contribution of SG&A Cost Efficiency

$$COEPS1_{i,t+1} = \alpha + \beta_1\, SG\&A_{i,t}^{sales\_fall} + \beta_2\, SG\&A_{i,t}^{sales\_fall} \cdot D_{i,t}^{sga\_low} + \beta_3\, SG\&A_{i,t}^{sales\_rise} + \beta_4\, SG\&A_{i,t}^{sales\_rise} \cdot D_{i,t}^{sga\_low}$$
$$+ \delta\, COEPS_{i,t} + \sum_{j=1}^{12} \gamma_j\, Other\ Signals_{i,j,t} + \varepsilon_{i,t+1}$$

Category	Coefficient	t-value	Mean adj. R^2
$SG\&A^{sales\_fall}$	0.012	0.83	
$SG\&A^{sales\_fall} \cdot D^{sga\_low}$	0.180	2.88	4.8%
$SG\&A^{sales\_rise}$	-0.034	-2.38	
$SG\&A^{sales\_rise} \cdot D^{sga\_low}$	0.102	1.41	

Table 3.5 (continued)

Table 3.5 presents the results of different analyses comparing the differentiation of the SG&A ratio signal by past SG&A cost efficiency ("cost efficiency model") and the direction of simultaneous changes in sales ("stickiness model"). The sample, variables, and procedures are depicted in Table 3.2, except for the SG&A ratio signal in the stickiness model. In this model, the SG&A signal is defined as follows:

$SG\&A_{i,t}^{sales\_fall} = \frac{SG\&A_{i,t}}{Sales_{i,t}} - \frac{SG\&A_{i,t-1}}{Sales_{i,t-1}}$ if sales decrease in the current period or 0 otherwise;

$SG\&A_{i,t}^{sales\_rise} = \frac{SG\&A_{i,t}}{Sales_{i,t}} - \frac{SG\&A_{i,t-1}}{Sales_{i,t-1}}$ if sales increase in the current period or 0 otherwise.

SG&A efficiency ($D_{i,t}^{sga\_low}$) = 1 if the firm-specific SG&A ratio was below or equal to the industry-average in period t - 1, 0 otherwise

Panel A shows the regression estimates of the SG&A ratio signal coefficients and t-values of the cost-efficient firms in the cost efficiency model and the firms exhibiting falling sales in the stickiness model.

Panel B illustrates the respective results of regressions on changes in operating earnings per share in the *year after next*.

Panel C shows the results of a simultaneous analysis of both differentiation approaches in *one* regression model, so as to reveal the incremental contribution of the differentiation by SG&A cost efficiency.

In a further step, I analyze the contribution of my differentiation by SG&A cost efficiency that is *incremental* to the segmentation by rising and falling sales. Therefore, I introduce interaction terms of the dummy variable D^{sga_low} of my forecast model with the SG&A ratio variables in the stickiness model.[62] Thus, I obtain the following regression model:

$$\begin{aligned} COEPS1_{i,t+1} = \alpha &+ \beta_1\, SG\&A_{i,t}^{sales\_fall} + \beta_2\, SG\&A_{i,t}^{sales\_fall} \cdot D_{i,t}^{sga\_low} \\ &+ \beta_3\, SG\&A_{i,t}^{sales\_rise} + \beta_4\, SG\&A_{i,t}^{sales\_rise} \cdot D_{i,t}^{sga\_low} \\ &+ \delta\, COEPS_{i,t} + \sum_{j=1}^{12} \gamma_j\, Other\ Signals_{i,j,t} + \varepsilon_{i,t+1} \end{aligned} \quad [3.6]$$

The empirical results in Panel C of Table 3.5 show that the positive influence of an increasing SG&A ratio is significantly higher if firms simultaneously exhibit falling sales and SG&A cost efficiency. The coefficient of SG&A cost-*efficient* firms with

[62] The dummy variable for SG&A cost efficiency takes the value 1 if a company belongs to the SG&A cost-efficient group and the value 0 if it belongs to the inefficient group.

falling sales significantly exceeds the coefficient for *inefficient* firms with falling sales (β_1) by 0.180 (β_2). The difference is statistically significant with a *t*-statistic of 2.88, underlining the incremental explanatory power of the differentiation by SG&A cost efficiency. This incremental explanatory power is less distinct in the analysis of firms with rising sales. The SG&A ratio coefficient of SG&A cost-inefficient firms with rising sales (β_3) is significantly negative. This implies that an increasing SG&A ratio negatively affects future profitability if firms simultaneously feature increasing sales and an insufficient control of their SG&A expenses. The coefficient for SG&A cost-*efficient* firms with rising sales exceeds that for *inefficient* firms with rising sales by 0.102 (β_4). However, this difference is not statistically significant at conventional levels (*t*-statistic: 1.41).

In conclusion, the positive impact of an increasing SG&A ratio on future profitability in periods of falling sales is much stronger for SG&A cost-efficient firms, indicating an intention to enhance future profitability. In contrast, an increasing SG&A ratio is a negative signal if sales rise and SG&A costs are managed inefficiently. This result underlines the incremental explanatory power of my approach and suggests that future research should take both differentiation approaches into account.

3.6 Sensitivity Analyses

3.6.1 Changes in the Segmentation of the Sample

I introduce two modifications of my differentiation condition. First, I require cost efficiency to be lasting, using the previous *two* periods, instead of *one* for the allocation. Companies are only assigned to the SG&A efficient category if their individual SG&A ratio was below or equal to the industry average in *both* previous periods and to the inefficient group otherwise. The analysis of this model yields the same conclusions with similar estimation results, as presented in Panel A of Table 3.6. Consequently, the implications derived from my model are not driven by singular occurrences of SG&A cost efficiency.

In a second variation of the separating condition, I differentiate the sample according to the *median* of the previous period's industry-specific SG&A ratio, instead of the *mean*. This method enforces a distribution of two equal shares of companies. As presented in Panel B of Table 3.6, this modification also does not qualitatively change my results. Thus, the alternative differentiation by the industry median confirms the conclusions drawn from the mean-based regression model.[63]

3.6.2 Impact on Earnings per Share

In order to facilitate the decomposition of the impact of the SG&A ratio into the effects on sales, cost of goods sold, and SG&A costs, my analysis focuses on the impact on *operating* earnings per share. However, the result of a positive impact of an increase in the SG&A ratio by SG&A cost-efficient firms also applies to *full* earnings per share, as shown in Panel C of Table 3.6. The SG&A ratio signal coefficient of the SG&A cost-inefficient companies is negative, but insignificant. I conclude from this empirical result that, with respect to full instead of operating earnings, for a subset of the SG&A cost-inefficient companies the traditional interpretation of cost inefficiency combined with negative consequences might apply, whereas diverse causes are possible for the rest. In total, this may lead to the insignificant influence.

All in all, changes in the differentiation by cost efficiency, as well as the consideration of additional components of earnings, confirm the main conclusions drawn from my analysis.[64]

---

[63] Following the robustness analysis in Anderson et al. [2007], I additionally recalculate my model on an industry-by-industry basis. The estimation results clearly confirm the conclusions drawn from the original regression.

[64] Additionally, I repeat all robustness tests for my second differentiation according to efficiency in the cost of goods sold. I arrive at the same conclusions as before.

Table 3.6: Robustness Tests

For Comparison: SG&A Ratio Signal Coefficients in the Original Analysis (as in Table 3.2)

$$COEPS1_{i,t+1} = \alpha + \beta_1\, SG\&A_{i,t}^{sga\_low} + \beta_2\, SG\&A_{i,t}^{sga\_high} + \delta\, COEPS_{i,t} + \sum_{j=1}^{12} \gamma_j\, Other\ Signals_{i,j,t} + \varepsilon_{i,t+1}$$

Variable	Coefficient	t-value	Model adj. R^2
$SG\&A^{sga\_low}$	0.157	4.13	4.5%
$SG\&A^{sga\_high}$	-0.019	-2.28	

Panel A: Consideration of an Additional Previous Period

$SG\&A_{i,t}^{sga\_low} = SG\&A\,Signal_{i,t}$ if the firm-specific SG&A ratio was below or equal to the industry-average in both previous periods or 0 otherwise

$SG\&A_{i,t}^{sga\_high} = SG\&A\,Signal_{i,t}$ if the firm-specific SG&A ratio was above the industry-average in at least one of the two previous periods or 0 otherwise

Variable	Coefficient	t-value	Mean adj. R^2
$SG\&A^{sga\_low}$	0.133	2.81	4.4%
$SG\&A^{sga\_high}$	-0.020	-1.77	

Panel B: Separation by the Industry Median

$SG\&A_{i,t}^{sga\_low} = SG\&A\,Signal_{i,t}$ if the firm-specific SG&A ratio was below or equal to the industry-*median* in the previous period or 0 otherwise

$SG\&A_{i,t}^{sga\_high} = SG\&A\,Signal_{i,t}$ if the firm-specific SG&A ratio was above the industry-*median* in the previous period or 0 otherwise

Variable	Coefficient	t-value	Mean adj. R^2
$SG\&A^{sga\_low}$	0.155	2.68	4.5%
$SG\&A^{sga\_high}$	-0.015	-2.00	

Panel C: One-Year-Ahead Changes in Earnings per Share

$$CEPS1_{i,t+1} = \alpha + \beta_1\, SG\&A_{i,t}^{sga\_low} + \beta_2\, SG\&A_{i,t}^{sga\_high} + \delta\, CEPS_{i,t} + \sum_{j=1}^{12} \gamma_j\, Other\,Signals_{i,j,t} + \varepsilon_{i,t+1}$$

with

$$CEPS1_{i,t+1} = \frac{Earnings\ per\ Share\,(\text{Compustat data item }\#54)_{i,t+1} - Earnings\ per\ Share_{i,t}}{P_{i,t-1}}$$

$$CEPS_{i,t+1} = \frac{Earnings\ per\ Share_{i,t} - Earnings\ per\ Share_{i,t-1}}{P_{i,t-1}}$$

Variable	Coefficient	t-value	Mean adj. R^2
$SG\&A^{sga\_low}$	0.499	3.73	7.5%
$SG\&A^{sga\_high}$	-0.009	-0.28	

Table 3.6 (continued)

Table 3.6 presents the results of different robustness tests, modifying the analysis introduced in Table 3.2. The sample, variables, and procedures are depicted in Table 3.2, except for the changes described here for each of the three tests.

Panel A shows the SG&A signal coefficients and t-values, as well as the mean adjusted R^2 of a regression analysis using an alternative segmentation approach. This alternative approach separates the sample by the last *two* periods' averages of the SG&A ratio, allocating companies to the below-average category if their individual SG&A ratio was below or equal to the industry average in both previous periods and to the above-average group otherwise.

Panel B presents the same statistics for another modification of the segmenting condition. In this case, the SG&A ratio signal is partitioned by the *median* of the last period's industry-specific SG&A ratio instead of the mean.

Panel C shows the results of a modification of the initial regression analyzing the impact on *full* earnings per share instead of *operating* earnings per share.

3.7 Conclusion

The information content of the SG&A ratio, as a key figure in fundamental analysis, proves to be more complex than the prevalent interpretation accommodates. According to the common view, high or rising values of this ratio are regarded as inefficiency in cost management, combined with negative impacts on future profitability. By contrast, recent research literature presents possible explanations for a positive effect of a rising SG&A ratio on future performance.

As the main contribution of this analysis, I show that it is crucial to differentiate between whether an increase in the SG&A ratio occurs with intent to enhance profitability or merely results from insufficient cost control. Using the past relationship of the individual SG&A ratio with its industry mean as a proxy for managerial SG&A cost control, I find a positive impact of a rising SG&A ratio on future operating earnings for SG&A cost-efficient firms and a negative impact for SG&A cost-inefficient firms. My study also contributes to the existing research by decomposing the impact of the SG&A ratio on future operating earnings. This disaggregation reveals that the positive effect of SG&A expenditures by SG&A cost-efficient firms results from a reduction in the future cost of goods sold. This finding indicates deliberate investments in process optimization and operational efficiency. Moreover, the positive impact of SG&A investments is exceptionally strong in the case of SG&A cost-efficient companies that have substantial room for improvement in their manufacturing processes. By means of targeted SG&A investments, these firms could improve their overall cost balance.

A limitation of my study is the fact that the aggregated reporting of SG&A costs defined by US-GAAP impedes the identification of the specific SG&A investments that enhance future profitability. In this regard, access to information concerning changes in individual components of SG&A cost would be helpful, in order to advance my analysis.

In conclusion, a differentiation by past SG&A cost efficiency enables a more appropriate assessment of the information content of the SG&A ratio. My inferences are important to different groups. First of all, managers can take advantage of my results. I advise them to compare their SG&A and cost-of-goods-sold efficiency with that of their competitors. Based on the results of this benchmarking, managers should be able to determine the potential benefits of SG&A investments. In addition, external users of financial statements, such as capital market investors or analysts, can benefit from my findings. By taking a firm's past cost efficiency into account, they are able to assess changes in the SG&A ratio beyond the prevalent interpretation.

4 Cost Stickiness and Analysts' Implied Cost Forecasts

The analysis of financial analysts' consideration of cost stickiness presented in the following chapter is based on my research study, which has been presented at the *34th Annual Congress of the European Accounting Association* in Rome, Italy, and at the *2011 Annual Meeting of the American Accounting Association* in Denver, Colorado.[65]

4.1 Introduction

As presented in Chapter 2, numerous studies show that costs are sticky, that is, they decrease less when sales fall than they increase when sales rise (e.g., ABJ; Calleja et al. [2006]). In this study, I combine cost stickiness with financial analysts' forecasts and hypothesize that analysts' implied cost forecasts (i.e., the differences between forecasted sales and forecasted earnings) disregard cost stickiness.[66]

The rationale underlying my hypothesis is earnings forecast optimism. Prior research shows that analysts' earnings forecasts are "externally" optimistic, that is, too high with respect to *actual earnings* (see Kothari [2001, 153-159] for a summary). I show that analysts' earnings forecasts are also "internally" optimistic, that is, too high with respect to *forecasted sales*. When earnings forecasts are too high with respect to forecasted sales, analysts underestimate the costs that a firm incurs when it reaches the forecasted sales level. Consequently, internal optimism in analysts' earnings forecasts implies that when analysts forecast rising (falling) sales, they underestimate (overestimate) the associated increase (decrease) in costs. When the combined effect of underestimating cost increases for rising sales and overestimating cost decreases for falling sales is strong enough to overcompensate cost stickiness, analysts' forecasts of costs that are in fact sticky can be "anti-sticky" (see Figure 4.1).

---

65 See Baumgarten et al. [2011].

66 Financial analysts routinely disclose their forecasts of sales and earnings, but not of costs. Consequently, I derive cost forecasts indirectly as the difference between forecasted sales and forecasted earnings. Hereafter, the term "cost forecasts" refers to these implied forecasts.

Figure 4.1: Cost Asymmetry

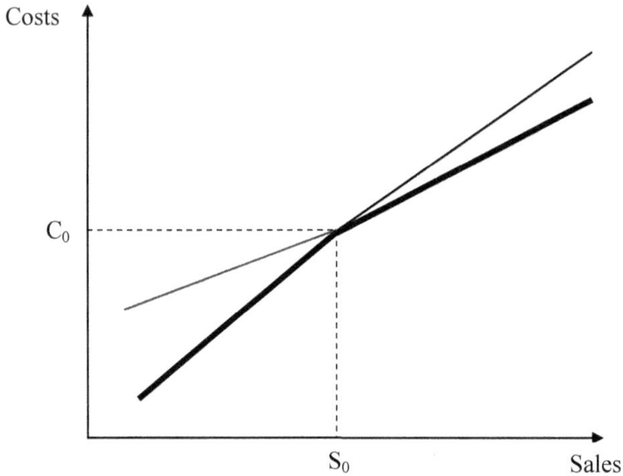

The figure shows that when analysts underestimate the increase in costs for rising sales and overestimate the decrease in costs for falling sales, analysts' forecasts of costs that are in fact sticky (thin cost function) can be anti-sticky (bold cost function). S_0 (C_0) is the current sales (cost) level.

In order to test my hypothesis that analysts' implied cost forecasts disregard cost stickiness, I use the cost stickiness model of ABJ and data from the Institutional Broker Estimate System (I/B/E/S). As presented in Chapter 2, ABJ's cost stickiness model regresses the logarithm of changes in costs on the logarithm of changes in sales, while discriminating between sales increases and decreases. My research design proceeds in two steps. In the first step, I estimate ABJ's model using actual changes in costs and sales of 4,681 firms covered by analysts. In the second step, I re-estimate the model, but replace actual changes in costs and sales with forecasted changes. The results confirm my hypothesis. Actual costs are sticky. On average, they decrease 0.72% per 1% actual decrease in sales and increase 0.82% per 1% actual increase in sales. Analysts' cost forecasts, on the other hand, are anti-sticky. On average, costs are forecasted to decrease 0.92% per 1% forecasted decrease in sales and forecasted to increase 0.74% per 1% forecasted increase in sales.

According to my results, analysts overestimate the percentage decrease in costs per 1% decrease in sales by 0.20 percentage points (0.92% vs. 0.72%), whereas they underestimate the percentage increase in costs per 1% increase in sales by only 0.08 percentage points (0.74% vs. 0.82%). I interpret this asymmetry as evidence that internal optimism in analysts' earnings forecasts is not merely a general byproduct of external optimism. Rather, internal optimism also seems to be caused by analysts who specifically underestimate the reason for sticky cost behavior, that is, who underestimate managerial hesitance to cut redundant resources. When sales fall, status considerations and loyalty towards longstanding employees induce managers to cut fewer resources than would be appropriate, given the new sales level (e.g., ABJ [2003, 49-50]). Analysts probably underestimate this behavior because, when generating their forecasts, analysts heavily rely on information provided by a firm's management (e.g., Ramnath et al. [2008, 41]). Managers, in turn, are unlikely to volunteer information to analysts that makes them (the managers) appear opportunistic or inefficient. Consequently, when analysts forecast falling sales, they are typically not well-informed about the possibility that managers will deliberately forgo or delay economically sensible resource cuts. This misinformation leads to earnings forecasts that are too high with respect to the forecasted sales level.

Prior research shows that external optimism declines as the announcement date approaches (e.g., Richardson et al. [1999]). Consistent with internal optimism experiencing a similar decline, I find that the disregard of cost stickiness in analysts' cost forecasts is restricted to early forecasts, that is, to those issued well before the announcement date. This finding indicates that analysts who initially underestimate managers' hesitance to cut redundant resources probably realize their mistake when, shortly before the announcement date, they still find no indications of asset sales or layoffs.

My analysis relates specifically to four recent studies examining analysts' forecasts. Firstly, my results shed new light on Weiss [2010, 1444 and 1462] who assumes that "analysts recognize cost behavior to a reasonable extent". I show that the answer to the question of whether analysts recognize cost behavior depends crucially on the forecast horizon. Late cost forecasts, that is, those issued shortly before the announcement date, do heed cost stickiness, whereas early cost forecasts, that is, those issued well before the announcement date, disregard cost stickiness.

Secondly, my study contradicts Kim and Prather-Kinsey [2010, 28] who suggest that analysts use "a proportionate cost model (PCM) in which they assume an equal growth rate for expenses as for sales". My results speak against analysts using such a PCM. In the second step of my research design, that is, in my second estimation of ABJ's cost stickiness model, I directly test the notion of analysts using a PCM by regressing the logarithm of forecasted changes in costs on the logarithm of forecasted changes in sales. If analysts did indeed use the PCM described by Kim and Prather-Kinsey [2010], the coefficient for this regression would be close to one. However, according to my results, the coefficient is 0.92 for forecasted sales decreases and 0.74 for forecasted sales increases.

Thirdly, my study offers a new perspective on Keung [2010] and Ertimur et al. [2011]. Both of these studies investigate the characteristics of analysts who issue disaggregated earnings forecasts to I/B/E/S, thus providing I/B/E/S not only with earnings forecasts, but also with sales forecasts. Keung [2010, 2049 and 2072] finds that analysts are more likely to supplement their earnings forecasts with sales forecasts, when they have "better information". Ertimur et al. [2011, 43 and 54] find that analysts who disaggregate tend to have a low reputation and high forecasting ability. Both studies conclude that competent analysts use the additional issuance of sales forecasts to signal their superior forecasting ability to the market. My results show that, despite the finding of Keung [2010] and Ertimur et al. [2011] that many disaggregating analysts possess good information and/or high forecasting ability, early earnings and sales forecasts on I/B/E/S are inconsistent, that is, they do not mirror the stickiness that characterizes actual cost behavior. This inconsistency should be of interest to both analysts and investors. Analysts should try to eradicate it. Investors should take it into account when they use I/B/E/S forecasts to make investment decisions.

The remainder of this chapter is structured as follows. Section 4.2 reviews the relevant literature and develops my hypotheses. Section 4.3 describes the research design and sample. Section 4.4 presents the results. Section 4.5 checks for robustness. Section 4.6 concludes.

4.2 Literature Review and Hypothesis Development

4.2.1 Cost Stickiness

As described in detail in Chapter 2 of this doctoral thesis, recent empirical research on cost behavior shows that costs decrease less when sales fall than they increase when sales rise. In a nutshell: Building on prior indications of an asymmetry in the cost reaction to activity-level increases and decreases (e.g., Noreen and Soderstrom [1997]), ABJ document and analyze this phenomenon, which they refer to as "cost stickiness" in a large-scale study that focuses on selling, general, and administrative (SG&A) costs. Subramaniam and Weidenmier [2003] find cost stickiness also for cost of goods sold (COGS) and total costs (i.e., for the sum of SG&A costs and COGS).

Recapitulated here for the development of my hypotheses, ABJ attribute cost stickiness to an asymmetry in managers' resource adjustments. When sales rise, managers readily increase a firm's resources to the extent necessary to accommodate additional sales. However, when sales fall, managers hesitate to cut the resources that have become redundant due to the lower sales level. ABJ [2003, 49-50] identify two main causes of managers' hesitance to cut redundant resources: *adjustment costs* and *managers' personal, self-interested considerations*. Adjustment costs include selling costs for assets, severance pay for dismissed employees, and training costs for new employees who have to be hired in subsequent periods when sales pick up again. Managers' personal, self-interested considerations include the desire to avoid loss of status when a division is downsized or the anguish of dismissing familiar employees. Chen et al. [2011] and Calleja et al. [2006] confirm the importance of self-interested managers for the emergence of sticky cost behavior by finding that cost stickiness is positively associated with managerial empire building incentives due to the agency problem and negatively associated with strong corporate governance.

4.2.2 Earnings Forecast Optimism

Numerous studies find that financial analysts' earnings forecasts exceed actual earnings. Most explanations of this optimism fall into four categories (Kothari [2001, 153-159]; Gu and Wu [2003, 6]). The *cognitive bias explanation* (e.g., Abarbanell and Bernard [1992]; Elgers and Lo [1994]) assumes that analysts forecast irrationally, that is, they commit systematic errors when processing public information. The *strategic reporting bias explanation* (e.g., Francis and Philbrick [1993]; Dugar and Nathan [1995]; Das et al. [1998]; Lim [2001]) assumes that analysts forecast rationally. However, they issue optimistic forecasts to generate additional revenue for their brokerage firms and to improve their relationship with managers. The *selection bias explanation* (McNichols and O'Brien [1997]) assumes that analysts forecast rationally and candidly. However, they publish their forecasts only when they consider them to be favorable. The *skewness bias explanation* (Gu and Wu [2003]) assumes that analysts forecast rationally, candidly, and unselectively. The optimism in their earnings forecasts results from skewness in the distribution of earnings and analysts' efforts to minimize absolute forecast error.

Richardson et al. [1999] find that the optimism in analysts' earnings forecasts declines or even reverses as the announcement date approaches. They interpret this finding as evidence that managers and analysts engage in an earnings-guidance game, in which analysts first issue optimistic earnings forecasts and then "walk down" their estimates to a level that managers can beat at the official earnings announcement. Managers particularly appreciate a beatable earnings forecast, that is, an opportunity to generate a positive earnings surprise, if they care about the firm's stock price level after the earnings announcement. Analysts, in turn, are more willing to issue a beatable earnings forecast if they wish to curry favor with managers in order to obtain or secure preferred information access (such as the opportunity to ask questions during conference calls). Consistent with these notions, Richardson et al. [2004] and Libby et al. [2008] find that the optimistic/pessimistic pattern in analysts' early and late earnings forecasts is more pronounced when managers are net sellers of stock after an earnings announcement or when analysts are not only interested in forecast accuracy, but also in maintaining a good relationship with a firm's management.

4.2.3 Hypotheses Development

The rationale behind my hypotheses is to combine cost stickiness with earnings forecast optimism. Mest and Plummer [2003] find that while analysts' earnings forecasts are optimistic, their sales forecasts are relatively unbiased. This asymmetry in the optimism of earnings and sales forecasts implies that earnings forecasts are not only "externally" optimistic, that is, too high with respect to actual earnings, but also "internally" optimistic, that is, too high with respect to forecasted sales. Internal optimism in earnings forecasts means that when analysts simultaneously forecast earnings and sales, the ratio of the two forecasts (the forecasted return on sales) is inappropriately high. Such an inflated forecasted return on sales implies that analysts underestimate the costs that a firm incurs when it reaches the forecasted sales level. Consequently, under the assumption that sales and costs move in the same direction ("co-movement"), internal optimism in analysts' earnings forecasts implies that when analysts forecast rising (falling) sales, they underestimate (overestimate) the associated increase (decrease) in costs. I assume that the combined effect of underestimating cost increases for rising sales and overestimating cost decreases for falling sales is strong enough to overcompensate or at least balance the asymmetry in the actual cost reaction to rising and falling sales (see Figure 4.1). Consequently, I hypothesize:

H1: Analysts' cost forecasts disregard cost stickiness.

According to the rationale underlying hypothesis H1, the disregard of cost stickiness in analysts' cost forecasts is driven by internal optimism in analysts' earnings forecasts, that is, by earnings forecasts that are too high with respect to forecasted sales. Internal optimism in analysts' earnings forecasts, in turn, can have several causes.

On the one hand, internal optimism may be a general byproduct of external optimism and thus be attributable to the forms of bias described in Section 4.2.2 (cognitive bias, strategic reporting bias, selection bias, skewness bias). I depict this concept by way of the strategic reporting bias. Take an analyst who forecasts a firm's sales and earnings (and thus implicitly also the firm's return on sales). The analyst aims to issue an externally optimistic earnings forecast to promote revenue-generating businesses for his brokerage firm. In order to do so, he can choose between three options:

i) He exaggerates the sales forecasts, but uses a realistic forecasted return on sales.

ii) He uses a realistic sales forecast, but exaggerates the forecasted return on sales.

iii) He exaggerates both the sales forecast and the forecasted return on sales.

All three options lead to an externally optimistic earnings forecast. However, when the analyst chooses option ii) or iii), the earnings forecast is, as a byproduct, also internally optimistic.

On the other hand, internal optimism may be caused by analysts who specifically underestimate the reason for sticky cost behavior, that is, who underestimate managers' hesitance to cut redundant resources. When analysts generate forecasts, they heavily rely on information provided by a firm's management (e.g., Lang and Lundholm [1996]; Bowen et al. [2002]). Managers, in turn, are generally reluctant to appear self-interested or inefficient. Consequently, when sales are expected to fall, managers prefer to promise analysts unrealistically high resource cuts than to inform them of their tendency to retain redundant resources due to status considerations or loyalty towards longstanding employees. Analysts who are gullible or do not want to openly question managers' honesty then issue earnings forecasts that are too high, given the expected sales decrease.

If internal optimism were only a general byproduct of external optimism, one would find that analysts overestimate the decrease in costs when sales fall and underestimate the increase in costs when sales rise. However, one would not find systematic differences in the intensities of the two misestimations. After all, none of the forms of bias that explain external optimism discriminates between earnings forecasts that are made for falling sales and earnings forecasts that are made for rising sales and thus, the magnitude of internal optimism that emerges as a byproduct of external optimism should not depend on the direction of the forecasted change in sales. In the above example, the probability of the business-seeking analyst exaggerating the forecasted return on sales should not depend on whether he predicts an increase or a decrease in sales.

On the other hand, if internal optimism were caused only by analysts who specifically underestimate managers' hesitance to cut redundant resources, one would find that analysts overestimate cost decreases for falling sales, but do not underestimate cost increases for rising sales. After all, when sales rise, there is generally no need for managers to cut unutilized resources.

I assume that both the forms of bias that explain external optimism and the underestimation of managers' hesitance to cut redundant resources cause internal optimism. Consequently, I hypothesize:

H2: Analysts overestimate the decrease in costs when sales fall and underestimate the increase in costs when sales rise. However, they overestimate cost decreases for falling sales to a greater extent than they underestimate cost increases for rising sales.

According to the rationale underlying hypothesis H2, internal optimism in analysts' earnings forecasts has two causes. The first cause are the forms of bias that explain external optimism. The second cause is analysts' underestimation of managerial hesitance to cut redundant resources. Both these causes are strong for early forecasts, but weak for late forecasts. Firstly, prior research shows that external optimism declines or even reverses as the announcement date approaches (see Section 4.2.2). Secondly, analysts who forecast falling sales and initially underestimate managerial hesitance to cut redundant resources probably realize their mistake when, shortly before the announcement date, they still find no indications of asset sales or layoffs. Due to this weakening in the causes of internal optimism over time, I hypothesize:

H3: The disregard of cost stickiness in analysts' cost forecasts is restricted to early forecasts, that is, to forecasts that are issued well before the announcement date.

One of the concepts underlying hypothesis H3 is that, towards the end of a forecasting period, analysts typically correct their initial underestimation of managerial hesitance to cut redundant resources when they find no indications of asset sales or layoffs. This raises the question of why analysts do not seem to learn from experience and gradually also stop underestimating managerial hesitance to cut redundant resources at the beginning of a forecasting period. A potential answer to this question lies in the fact that for most firms, decreasing sales (and thus opportunities for analysts to observe managerial resistance to resource cuts) are rare events. In my sample, only about 30 percent of firms have more than one observation of a decrease in sales during the ten year sample period from 2000 to 2009. Consequently, learning about manager reactions to sales decreases would, in most cases, require analysts to generalize from experiences with the management of one particular firm in one particular period to other firms in other periods. Analysts not making such generalizations will often regard the management reaction to a sales decrease at a particular firm in a particular period as a unique event that has little explanatory power for future management reactions to sales decreases at other firms. For example, an analyst who had observed that Apple's management did not cut redundant resources when Apple's sales declined in 2001, will not automatically have expected Microsoft's management similarly not to cut redundant resources when Microsoft's sales fell in 2009. Consequently, the rarity of sales decreases for most firms, combined with analysts not generalizing between firms, might impede the learning process that could gradually make analysts also stop underestimating managerial hesitance to cut redundant resources at the beginning of a forecasting period.

My main hypothesis H1 differs from the research questions of prior studies examining cost stickiness. Prior studies hypothesize that cost stickiness is smaller for specific firms (e.g., firms with excess capacity) or specific cost categories (e.g., costs in non-core activities).[67] My study, on the other hand, hypothesizes that cost stickiness disappears when one replaces actual with forecasted costs and sales. In deriving my hypotheses, I combine cost stickiness with earnings forecast optimism. Thus, I contribute to integrating management and financial accounting research topics, a research gap recently identified by Weiss [2010].

---

67 See, e.g., Balakrishnan et al. [2004] and Balakrishnan and Gruca [2008].

4.3 Research Design and Sample

4.3.1 Research Design

My research design is based on the established cost stickiness model of ABJ. As explained in Chapter 2, this model regresses the logarithm of changes in costs on the logarithm of changes in sales and a dummy interaction term that discriminates between sales increases and decreases. I estimate ABJ's model three times. In the first estimation, I use *actual* changes in costs and sales. In the second estimation, I use *early forecasts* of changes in costs and sales. In the third estimation, I use *late forecasts* of changes in costs and sales. Analysts generally do not disclose their cost forecasts. Consequently, I calculate both actual and forecasted costs implicitly as the difference between sales and earnings.[68]

The first estimation checks whether the actual costs of the firms in my sample, that is, the actual costs of firms under analyst coverage and included in the I/B/E/S database, are sticky. By means of this preliminary analysis, I wish to rule out finding no stickiness in analysts' cost forecasts, not because analysts' forecasts disregard cost stickiness (as I hypothesize), but because the actual costs of the firms for which the cost forecasts were made are not sticky. The regression model for the first estimation is the following:

$$\log\left[\frac{Costs_{i,t}}{Costs_{i,t-1}}\right] = \beta_0 + \beta_1 \cdot \log\left[\frac{Sales_{i,t}}{Sales_{i,t-1}}\right] + \beta_2 \cdot Decrease\_Dummy_{i,t} \cdot \log\left[\frac{Sales_{i,t}}{Sales_{i,t-1}}\right] + \varepsilon_{i,t} \qquad [4.1]$$

where

$$Costs_{i,t} = Sales_{i,t} - Earnings_{i,t}$$

$Decrease\_Dummy_{i,t} = 1$ when $Sales_{i,t} < Sales_{i,t-1}$, 0 otherwise

$Sales_{i,t}$ are the actual sales of firm i in period t as reported in I/B/E/S. $Earnings_{i,t}$ are the actual earnings of firm i in year t. They are calculated by multiplying actual earnings per share (EPS) from I/B/E/S by the number of *common shares used to*

68 Calculating costs as the difference between sales and earnings implies that I analyze cost stickiness for "total costs", i.e., for a comprehensive cost figure that includes both SG&A costs and COGS (see Subramiam and Weidenmier [2003] and Calleja et al. [2006]).

calculate earnings per share from Compustat.[69] The dummy variable $Decrease\_Dummy_{i,t}$ is 1 when actual sales decrease and 0 when actual sales increase. Thus, the coefficient β_1 in model [4.1] measures the average percentage increase in actual costs for a one percent increase in actual sales, whereas the sum of the coefficients β_1 and β_2 in model [4.1] measures the percentage decrease in actual costs for a one percent decrease in actual sales. If actual costs are sticky, that is, if actual costs decrease less when actual sales fall than they increase when actual sales rise, β_2 will be negative (conditional on β_1 being positive). Accordingly, the empirical hypothesis for actual costs being sticky is $\beta_2 < 0$ in model [4.1].

The second estimation tests my hypothesis that analysts' cost forecasts disregard cost stickiness. This estimation replicates the analysis of model [4.1] but replaces actual changes in costs and sales with early forecasts of changes in costs and sales. The regression model is now as follows:

$$\log\left[\frac{\widehat{Costs}_{i,t}}{Costs_{i,t-1}}\right] = \beta_0 + \beta_1 \cdot \log\left[\frac{\widehat{Sales}_{i,t}}{Sales_{i,t-1}}\right] + \beta_2 \cdot \overline{Decrease\_Dummy}_{i,t} \cdot \log\left[\frac{\widehat{Sales}_{i,t}}{Sales_{i,t-1}}\right] + \varepsilon_{i,t} \qquad [4.2]$$

where

$$\widehat{Costs}_{i,t} = \widehat{Sales}_{i,t} - \widehat{Earnings}_{i,t}$$

$$\overline{Decrease\_Dummy}_{i,t} = 1 \text{ if } \widehat{Sales}_{i,t} < Sales_{i,t-1}, \text{ 0 otherwise}$$

$\widehat{Sales}_{i,t}$ is the early consensus forecast of the sales of firm i in year t. The early consensus forecast is the mean of all individual I/B/E/S sales forecasts outstanding on the 30th day subsequent to the prior year's earnings announcement. $\widehat{Earnings}_{i,t}$ is the early consensus forecast of the earnings of firm i in year t and is calculated by multiplying the early consensus forecasts of EPS with the number of *common shares used to calculate earnings per share* from Compustat. The early consensus forecast of EPS is the mean of all individual I/B/E/S EPS forecasts outstanding on the 30th day

[69] I/B/E/S contains far more earnings observations on a per-share basis than on a non-per share basis. Consequently, I calculate actual (forecasted) earnings by multiplying actual (forecasted) earnings per share by the number of shares used to calculate earnings per share, in order to maximize the size of my sample. However, I obtain similar results and identical conclusions when I directly use actual and forecasted earnings on a non-per share basis.

subsequent to the prior year's earnings announcement. Because the value of $\overline{Decrease\_Dummy_{i,t}}$ is 0 when sales are forecasted to rise, the coefficient β_1 in model [4.2] measures the average forecasted percentage increase in costs for a one percent forecasted increase in sales. Because the value of $\overline{Decrease\_Dummy_{i,t}}$ is 1 when sales are forecasted to fall, the sum of the coefficients β_1 and β_2 in model [4.2] measures the average forecasted percentage decrease in costs for a one percent forecasted decrease in sales. If cost forecasts are not sticky, β_2 will be non-negative (conditional on β_1 being positive). Accordingly, the empirical hypothesis for analysts' cost forecasts disregarding cost stickiness is $\beta_2 \geq 0$ in model [4.2].

The third estimation tests my hypothesis that the disregard of cost stickiness in analysts' cost forecasts is restricted to early forecasts. This estimation replicates the analysis of model [4.2], but replaces early forecasts of changes in costs and sales with late forecasts. Late consensus forecasts of sales and EPS are calculated as the mean of all individual I/B/E/S forecasts outstanding immediately prior to the current year's earnings announcement. The empirical hypothesis for the disregard of cost stickiness in analysts' cost forecasts being restricted to early forecasts is $\beta_2 < 0$ in the replicated version of model [4.2].

4.3.2 Sample and Descriptive Statistics

I obtain sales and EPS forecasts from the I/B/E/S detail file and actual values from the I/B/E/S actuals file. The I/B/E/S detail file contains the forecasts made by individual analysts. For each firm and each fiscal year, I construct early and late consensus forecasts of sales and EPS. Early consensus forecasts are based on forecasts outstanding at the beginning of the year. They are computed as the mean of all individual forecasts outstanding on the 30th day subsequent to the prior year's earnings announcement. Late consensus forecasts, on the other hand, are based on forecasts outstanding at the end of the year. They are computed as the mean of all individual forecasts outstanding immediately prior to the current year's earnings announcement. In order to avoid stale forecasts in the computation of early (late) consensus forecasts, I exclude outstanding individual forecasts whose last review takes place more than 90 days before the 30th day subsequent to the prior year's earnings announcement (before the current year's earnings announcement). Furthermore, in order to ensure comparability of the four consensus forecasts, I exclude individual sales (EPS) forecasts for which no corresponding individual EPS (sales) forecast is available from the same analyst and, similarly, I exclude individual early (late) forecasts for which no corresponding individual late (early) forecast is available from the same analyst. Accordingly, in each individual firm-year, all four consensus forecasts are based on an identical number of analysts' forecasts.[70]

Having computed comparable early and late consensus forecasts of sales and EPS, I convert actual and forecasted EPS to total earnings by multiplying them by the number of common shares used to calculate earnings per share from Compustat. If most analysts forecast *primary* EPS, I multiply actual and forecasted EPS by "common shares used to calculate earnings per share - basic" (mnemonic *cshpr*, data item #54). On the other hand, if most analysts forecast *diluted* EPS, I multiply actual and forecasted EPS by "common shares used to calculate earnings per share - fully diluted" (mnemonic *cshfd*, data item #171). I then calculate actual (forecasted) costs as the difference between actual (forecasted) sales and actual (forecasted) earnings. At this point, each firm-year in my sample has actual values as well as comparable early and late consensus forecasts of costs and sales. Next, I implement the following restrictions:

- I exclude non-US firms and observations from before 2000 or after 2009. I choose the time window 2000-2009 for my analysis in order to ensure that each year has at least 1,000 usable observations.
- I exclude observations where, in the current or preceding year, the ratio of actual costs to actual sales is less than 0.1 or greater than 10.[71]
- In order to ensure that sample statistics for forecast errors or regression results are not influenced by a small number of extreme observations, I trim the remaining data by deleting observations where
  i) the early or late percentage forecast error for earnings or sales,
  ii) the actual change in costs or sales, or
  iii) the early or late forecast of the change in costs or sales

  fall into the top or bottom 0.5% of its respective distribution.[72]

[70] A similar procedure for creating comparable consensus forecasts is used by Givoly et al. [2009].

[71] See Banker et al. [2011c] for a similar requirement.

After implementing all of the above restrictions, my final sample consists of 20,230 firm-years from 4,681 different firms. Table 4.1 reports summary statistics for this sample.

Panel A shows that analysts' average early consensus forecast of a firm's change in sales of 14.3% is almost identical to the average actual increase in sales of 14.2%, whereas analysts' average early consensus forecast of a firm's change in costs is 2.7 percentage points lower than the average actual increase in costs of 14.1%. Analysts' average late consensus forecasts of changes in sales and costs, on the other hand, are both relatively similar to average actual changes.

Panel B shows that, consistent with Mest and Plummer [2003], my sample exhibits early consensus forecasts of earnings that are too high with respect to actual earnings and early consensus forecasts of sales that are relatively unbiased with respect to actual sales. The average early percentage forecast error for earnings is 0.397, whereas the average early percentage forecast error for sales is only 0.027. Furthermore, Panel B shows that, consistent with Richardson et al. [1999], external optimism in analysts' earnings forecasts declines as the announcement date approaches. As in Richardson et al. [1999, 9-10], the mean late percentage forecast error for earnings is close to zero, but still optimistic (positive), whereas the median late percentage forecast error is pessimistic (negative).[73]

The statistics in Panels A and B are coherent. At the beginning of the year, analysts issue earnings forecasts that are optimistic and sales forecasts that are unbiased (Panel B). When one combines unbiased sales forecasts with optimistic earnings forecasts to calculate implied cost forecasts, these cost forecasts are likewise optimistic, that is, too low (Panel A). Towards the end of the year, the optimism in analysts' earnings forecasts declines (Panel B) and since analysts' sales forecasts remain unbiased, this decline in optimism also applies to implied cost forecasts (Panel A).

---

[72] Truncating my sample at the 0.5 level emulates ABJ and Banker [2011c]. Note that more extensive truncating does not change my results qualitatively (see the robustness tests in Section 4.5).

[73] Note that Richardson et al. [1999] calculate forecast errors as the scaled differences between actual and forecasted values, whereas I calculate forecast errors as the scaled differences between forecasted and actual values. Consequently, when comparing the two studies, positive and negative signs for forecast errors require reverse interpretations.

Table 4.1: Descriptive Statistics on Analysts' Forecasts

Panel A: Distribution of Actual and Forecasted Changes in Sales and Costs

		Mean	Standard Deviation	Q1	Median	Q3
Actuals	$\frac{Sales_{i,t}}{Sales_{i,t-1}}$	1.142	0.313	0.994	1.093	1.224
	$\frac{Costs_{i,t}}{Costs_{i,t-1}}$	1.141	0.305	0.997	1.092	1.220
Early Consensus Forecasts	$\frac{\widehat{Sales}_{i,t}}{Sales_{i,t-1}}$	1.143	0.264	1.029	1.095	1.200
	$\frac{\widehat{Costs}_{i,t}}{Costs_{i,t-1}}$	1.114	0.233	1.016	1.081	1.178
Late Consensus Forecasts	$\frac{\widehat{Sales}_{i,t}}{Sales_{i,t-1}}$	1.136	0.310	0.993	1.089	1.218
	$\frac{\widehat{Costs}_{i,t}}{Costs_{i,t-1}}$	1.131	0.292	0.995	1.088	1.212

Panel B: Distribution of Earnings and Sales Forecast Errors

		Mean	Standard Deviation	Q1	Median	Q3
Early Forecast Error	Earnings	0.397	1.542	-0.106	0.019	0.358
	Sales	0.027	0.197	-0.055	0.002	0.071
Late Forecast Error	Earnings	0.023	0.381	-0.045	-0.009	0.020
	Sales	-0.001	0.075	-0.013	-0.002	0.007

Panel A presents descriptive statistics on actual and forecasted changes in sales and costs. Actual [forecasted] costs are the difference between actual [forecasted] sales and actual [forecasted] earnings. Actual [forecasted] earnings are actual [forecasted] earnings per share (EPS) times *common shares used to calculate earnings per share* (Compustat data item #54 or #171). Early [late] forecasts of sales and EPS are consensus forecasts calculated as the mean of all individual forecasts (from the I/B/E/S detail file) outstanding on the 30th day subsequent to the prior year's earnings announcement [outstanding immediately prior to the current year's earnings announcement]. In the calculation of early [late] consensus forecasts of EPS (sales), an individual EPS (sales) forecasts is excluded when i) its last review takes place more than 90 days before the 30th day subsequent to the prior year's earnings announcement (more than 90 days before the current year's earnings announcement), ii) no corresponding individual early [late] sales (EPS) forecast is available from the same analyst, iii) no corresponding individual late [early] EPS (sales) forecast is available from the same analyst. Actual sales and EPS are from the I/B/E/S actuals file. The sample covers the period 2000-2009.

Table 4.1 (continued)

Non-US firms and observations, for which in the current or preceding year, the ratio of actual costs to actual sales is less than 0.1 or greater than 10 are excluded. Furthermore, observations that are extreme with respect to early or late percentage forecast errors for earnings or sales or with respect to actual or forecasted changes in costs and sales are truncated at the 0.5% level. The sample consists of 20,230 firm-years from 4,681 different firms.

Panel B presents descriptive statistics on early and late forecast errors for earnings and sales in my sample. Firm-year specific earnings and sales forecast errors are calculated as follows:

$$FEear_{i,t} = \frac{\widehat{Earnings}_{i,t} - Earnings_{i,t}}{|Earnings_{i,t}|} \qquad FEsal_{i,t} = \frac{\widehat{Sales}_{i,t} - Sales_{i,t}}{Sales_{i,t}}$$

4.4 Results

Table 2 presents OLS estimation results for regression model [4.1] and for the two versions of regression model [4.2]. I tested each model for heteroscedasticity by performing White's [1980] test and for multicollinearity by computing variance inflation factors (vifs). The hypothesis of heteroscedasticity was always rejected at the 1 percent level and all vifs were close to 1, well below common cutoffs.

The results in Table 4.2 confirm my hypotheses. In model [4.1], that is, in the model using *actual* values, the coefficient β_2 is negative (-0.101) and significantly different from zero at the 1% level (t-statistic -8.62). This finding shows that actual costs of firms under analyst coverage are indeed sticky. On average, they increase 0.82% per 1% actual increase in sales (β_1) and decrease 0.72% per 1% actual decrease in sales ($\beta_1 + \beta_2$). In the first version of model [4.2], that is, in the version using *early forecasts*, the coefficient β_2 is positive (0.184) and significant at the 1% level (t-statistic 14.96). This finding shows that early cost forecasts are anti-sticky. At the beginning of the year, costs are, on average, forecasted to increase 0.74% per 1% forecasted increase in sales (β_1) and forecasted to decrease 0.92% per 1% forecasted decrease in sales ($\beta_1 + \beta_2$). In the second version of model [4.2], that is, in the version using *late forecasts*, the coefficient β_2 is negative (-0.048) and significant at the 1% level (t-statistic -4.31). This finding shows that late cost forecasts are sticky. At the end of the year, costs are, on average, forecasted to increase 0.81% per 1% forecasted increase in sales (β_1) and forecasted to decrease 0.76% per 1% forecasted decrease in sales ($\beta_1 + \beta_2$).

The discrepancy between a significantly negative value for β_2 in model [4.1] and a significantly positive value for β_2 in the *first* version of model [4.2] shows that analysts' cost forecasts disregard cost stickiness (hypothesis H1). However, the conformity between the significantly negative values for β_2 in model [4.1] and in the *second* version of model [4.2] shows that the disregard of cost stickiness in analysts' cost forecasts is restricted to early forecasts (hypothesis H3). According to my results for model [4.1] and for the first version of model [4.2], analysts overestimate the percentage decrease in costs per 1% decrease in sales by 0.20 percentage points (0.92% vs. 0.72%), whereas they underestimate the percentage increase in costs per 1% increase in sales by only 0.08 percentage points (0.74% vs. 0.82%). This finding shows that analysts both overestimate the decrease in costs when sales fall and underestimate the increase in costs when sales rise. However, they overestimate cost decreases for falling sales more than they underestimate cost increases for rising sales (hypothesis H2).[74]

The confirmation of hypothesis H2 supports the notion that internal optimism in analysts' earnings forecasts (as the driver of analysts' cost forecasts' disregard of cost stickiness) is not merely a general byproduct of external optimism, but also caused by analysts who specifically underestimate the reason for sticky cost behavior, that is, who underestimate managerial hesitance to cut redundant resources. Many of the potential reasons for managerial hesitance to cut redundant resources are based on the notion that managers allow their business decisions to be affected by personal, self-interested considerations (e.g., reluctance to accept a loss of status, dismiss longstanding employees, or to revise overambitious past investment decisions). Consequently, when sales are expected to fall and managers inform analysts about their intention to retain redundant resources, they are likely to be regarded as self-interested or inefficient. In order to avoid such unfavorable attributes, managers prefer to promise analysts substantial resource cuts than disclose their tendency to retain unutilized resources. Analysts, in turn, rely on managers as a major source of information and thus, managerial unwillingness to communicate their tendency to retain unutilized resources translates into analysts' earnings forecasts that are too high, given the expected sales decrease.

---

[74] Additional statistical tests confirm that the difference in the extent to which analysts underestimate cost increases for rising sales and overestimate cost decreases for falling sales is significant at the 1% level.

Table 4.2: Regression of Changes in Costs on Changes in Sales

Panel A: Analysis of Cost Stickiness in Actual Data

$$\log\left[\frac{Costs_{i,t}}{Costs_{i,t-1}}\right] = \beta_0 + \beta_1 \cdot \log\left[\frac{Sales_{i,t}}{Sales_{i,t-1}}\right] + \beta_2 \cdot Decrease\_Dummy_{i,t} \cdot \log\left[\frac{Sales_{i,t}}{Sales_{i,t-1}}\right] + \varepsilon_{i,t} \qquad [4.1]$$

$Costs_{i,t} = Sales_{i,t} - Earnings_{i,t}$

$Decrease\_Dummy_{i,t} = 1$ if $Sales_{i,t} < Sales_{i,t-1}$, 0 otherwise

	Coefficient	t-value	adj. R²	N
β_0	0.015	11.28		
β_1	0.818	149.55	66.21%	20,230
β_2	-0.101	-8.62		

Panel B: Analysis of Cost Stickiness in Analysts' Forecasts

$$\log\left[\frac{\widehat{Costs}_{i,t}}{Costs_{i,t-1}}\right] = \beta_0 + \beta_1 \cdot \log\left[\frac{\widehat{Sales}_{i,t}}{Sales_{i,t-1}}\right] + \beta_2 \cdot \overline{Decrease\_Dummy}_{i,t} \cdot \log\left[\frac{\widehat{Sales}_{i,t}}{Sales_{i,t-1}}\right] + \varepsilon_{i,t} \qquad [4.2]$$

$\widehat{Costs}_{i,t} = \widehat{Sales}_{i,t} - \widehat{Earnings}_{i,t}$

$\overline{Decrease\_Dummy}_{i,t} = 1$ if $\widehat{Sales}_{i,t} < Sales_{i,t-1}$, 0 otherwise

	Early Forecasts				Late Forecasts			
	Coefficient	t-value	adj. R²	N	Coefficient	t-value	adj. R²	N
β_0	0.011	9.33			0.014	11.07		
β_1	0.737	145.11	65.71%	20,230	0.810	153.03	68.34%	20,230
β_2	0.184	14.96			-0.048	-4.31		

The table presents OLS estimation results for regressions of actual (forecasted) changes in costs on actual (forecasted) changes in sales, while discriminating between actual (forecasted) sales increases and decreases. The sample is described in Table 4.1.

Panel A reports the results for the regression of actual changes in costs on actual changes in sales (model [1]). $Sales_{i,t}$ are the actual sales of firm *i* in period *t* as reported in I/B/E/S. $Earnings_{i,t}$ are the actual earnings of firm *i* in period *t*. They are calculated by multiplying actual earnings per share (EPS) from I/B/E/S by *common shares used to calculate earnings per share* (Compustat data item #54 or #171).

Table 4.2 (continued)

Panel B reports the results for the regression of forecasted changes in costs on forecasted changes in sales (model [4.2]). The table discriminates between regression results for early and late forecasts. $\widehat{Sales}_{i,t}$ is the consensus forecast of the sales of firm i in year t. In the regression using early (late) forecasts, it is calculated as the mean of all individual I/B/E/S sales forecasts outstanding on the 30th day subsequent to the prior year's earnings announcement (outstanding immediately prior to the current year's earnings announcement). $\widehat{Earnings}_{i,t}$ is the consensus forecast of the earnings of firm i in year t. It is calculated by multiplying the consensus forecast of EPS by *common shares used to calculate earnings per share* (Compustat data item #54 or #171). In the regression using early (late) forecasts, the consensus forecast of EPS is the mean of all individual I/B/E/S EPS forecasts outstanding on the 30th day subsequent to the prior year's earnings announcement (outstanding immediately prior to the current year's earnings announcement).

4.5 Sensitivity Analyses

In order to check the robustness of the results described in Section 4.4, I modify my analysis in eight distinct respects. Table 4.3 reports the results that I obtain for each of these modifications. These results indicate that neither changes in my analytical approach, nor sample restrictions, change the conclusions drawn from my original analysis.

4.5.1 More Extensive Data Trimming

In order to further test for potential distortion caused by outliers, I truncate extreme forecast errors and regression variables not at the 0.5% level, but at the 5% level. This more extensive data trimming does not change my results qualitatively (Panel A of Table 4.3).

4.5.2 Median Consensus Forecasts

I use *median* instead of the *mean* consensus forecasts of costs and sales. The analysis of this approach yields the same conclusions and similar estimation results (Panel B of Table 4.3).

4.5.3 Problematic Cost Components

In my original analysis, I calculate both actual and forecasted costs indirectly from I/B/E/S data, as the difference between (forecasted) sales and (forecasted) earnings. Consequently, my costs include not only cost of goods sold (cogs) and selling, general, and administrative costs (SG&A), but also cost components that are typically excluded from an analysis of cost stickiness, since their magnitude hardly depends on the sales level (e.g., depreciation, interest expenses, or taxes). In order to reduce the effect of these problematic cost components, I exclude observations where, in the current and preceding year, actual costs (as I calculate them) differ by more than 20% from the sum of COGS and SG&A costs as reported in Compustat (mnemonics *cogs* and *xsga*, data items #41 and #189). Replicating my analysis under this requirement leads to qualitatively identical results (Panel C of Table 4.3). Note that in this robustness check, my results for model [4.1] (actual costs) are similar to those obtained by Subramaniam and Weidenmier [2003], who test for cost stickiness in actual total costs that are calculated directly from Compustat data as the sum of COGS and SG&A costs.

4.5.4 Individual Forecasts

I use individual instead of consensus forecasts of costs and sales. The sample for this robustness test consists of all individual cost and sales forecasts used in the construction of the consensus forecasts for the original sample. Using individual instead of consensus forecasts increases the number of observations, but once again, does not change my conclusions qualitatively (Panel D of Table 4.3).

4.5.5 Industrial Firms

In his analysis of cost stickiness, Weiss [2010] focuses on industrial firms (SIC codes 2000–3999), in order to increase the comparability of the sample firms. When I emulate this focus and restrict my sample to industrial firms, my results remain qualitatively unchanged (Panel E of Table 4.3).

Table 4.3: Robustness Tests

For comparison: Original Analysis (see Table 4.2)

	Actuals (model [4.1])		Early Forecasts (model [4.2])		Late Forecasts (model [4.2])	
	Coefficient	t-value	Coefficient	t-value	Coefficient	t-value
β_0	0.015	11.28	0.011	9.33	0.014	11.07
β_1	0.818	149.55	0.737	145.11	0.810	153.03
β_2	-0.101	-8.62	0.184	14.96	-0.048	-4.31
adj. R^2	66.21%		65.71%		68.34%	
N	20,230		20,230		20,230	

Panel A: More Extensive Data Trimming

	Actuals		Early Forecasts		Late Forecasts	
	Coefficient	t-value	Coefficient	t-value	Coefficient	t-value
β_0	0.011	12.20	0.006	7.54	0.011	12.63
β_1	0.857	172.41	0.828	172.25	0.857	174.58
β_2	-0.058	-3.98	0.052	2.73	-0.058	-4.04
adj. R^2	77.88%		75.17%		78.34%	
N	14,013		14,013		14,013	

Panel B: Median Consensus Forecasts

	Actuals		Early Forecasts		Late Forecasts	
	Coefficient	t-value	Coefficient	t-value	Coefficient	t-value
β_0	0.015	11.28	0.009	8.39	0.014	10.78
β_1	0.818	149.55	0.743	145.73	0.810	152.43
β_2	-0.101	-8.62	0.167	13.65	-0.051	-4.56
adj. R^2	66.21%		65.74%		68.21%	
N	20,230		20,230		20,230	

Panel C: Problematic Cost Components

	Actuals		Early Forecasts		Late Forecasts	
	Coefficient	t-value	Coefficient	t-value	Coefficient	t-value
β_0	0.009	8.72	0.011	11.63	0.009	8.90
β_1	0.856	185.46	0.781	174.94	0.858	187.91
β_2	-0.091	-9.55	0.122	10.94	-0.088	-9.38
adj. R^2	83.99%		80.78%		84.32%	
N	12,304		12,304		12,304	

Table 4.3 (continued)

Panel D: Individual Forecasts

	Actuals		Early Forecasts		Late Forecasts	
	Coefficient	t-value	Coefficient	t-value	Coefficient	t-value
β_0	0.015	22.97	0.012	21.44	0.016	25.41
β_1	0.823	300.56	0.765	286.91	0.818	301.13
β_2	-0.086	-15.08	0.129	22.86	-0.024	-4.46
adj. R^2	69.78%		69.03%		71.52%	
N	71,353		71,353		71,353	

Panel E: Industrial Firms

	Actuals		Early Forecasts		Late Forecasts	
	Coefficient	t-value	Coefficient	t-value	Coefficient	t-value
β_0	0.017	7.97	0.020	11.21	0.017	8.32
β_1	0.742	89.09	0.643	82.03	0.740	90.69
β_2	-0.112	-6.56	0.071	3.62	-0.101	-6.05
adj. R^2	64.45%		57.77%		65.22%	
N	8,110		8,110		8,110	

Panel F (Part 1): Clustered Standard Errors

	Actuals		Early Forecasts		Late Forecasts	
	Coefficient	t-value	Coefficient	t-value	Coefficient	t-value
β_0	0.031	6.51	0.022	4.90	0.021	4.41
β_1	0.811	75.52	0.734	57.04	0.805	75.70
β_2	-0.108	-4.87	0.187	6.86	-0.053	-2.43
adj. R^2	66.56%		65.86%		68.55%	
N	20,230		20,230		20,230	

Panel F (Part 2): Fama/MacBeth [1973] Regression

	Actuals		Early Forecasts		Late Forecasts	
	Coefficient	t-value	Coefficient	t-value	Coefficient	t-value
β_0	0.016	3.49	0.012	3.71	0.015	3.32
β_1	0.811	73.55	0.728	46.91	0.804	64.14
β_2	-0.142	-3.57	0.226	4.12	-0.057	-1.17
adj. R^2	66.19%		65.69%		68.35%	
N	20,230		20,230		20,230	

Table 4.3 (continued)

Panel G: Main Effect of Decrease Dummy

	Actuals		Early Forecasts		Late Forecasts	
	Coefficient	**t-value**	**Coefficient**	**t-value**	**Coefficient**	**t-value**
β_0	0.020	12.31	0.015	11.95	0.020	12.94
β_1	0.807	136.485	0.723	135.68	0.796	139.64
β_2	-0.123	-9.86	0.135	9.85	-0.076	-6.36
Decrease Dummy	-0.016	-5.14	-0.023	-8.08	-0.020	-6.68
adj. R^2	66.26%		65,83%		68,42%	
N	20,230		20,230		20,230	

Panel H: Experienced Analysts

	Actuals		Early Forecasts		Late Forecasts	
	Coefficient	**t-value**	**Coefficient**	**t-value**	**Coefficient**	**t-value**
β_0	0.011	8.00	0.006	5.27	0.009	6.72
β_1	0.836	118.91	0.781	111.72	0.842	122.44
β_2	-0.063	-4.68	0.130	9.25	-0.047	-3.69
adj. R^2	71.17%		69.60%		73.14%	
N	12,206		12,206		12,206	

Table 4.3 presents the results of different robustness tests, each of which modifies the analysis described in Table 4.2. The sample, variables and procedures are described in Tables 4.1 and 4.2, except for the specific changes made by the robustness tests.

Panel A shows the results when extreme regression variables are not truncated at the 0.5% level, but at the 5% level.

Panels B shows the results when I use median instead of mean consensus forecasts of costs and sales.

Panel C shows the results when I exclude observations for which, in the current and preceding year, actual costs as I calculate them, differ by more than 20% from the sum of cost of goods sold and selling, general, and administrative costs, as reported in Compustat (data items #41 and #189).

Panel D shows the results when I use individual instead of consensus forecasts of costs and sales.

Panel E shows the results when I restrict the sample to industrial firms (SIC codes 2000–3999).

Panel F shows the results when, instead of using standard OLS regression, I estimate my models via OLS regression with standard errors clustered by firm and year dummies (part 1) or via Fama/MacBeth [1973] regression (part 2).

Panel G shows the results when I include the main effect of the decrease dummy.

Panel H shows the results when I restrict my analysis to forecasts made by analysts with at least three years of firm-specific forecasting experience

4.5.6 Clustered Standard Errors or Fama-MacBeth [1973] Regression

In my original analysis, I follow ABJ and estimate their cost stickiness model using standard OLS regression. Chen et al. [2011] and Banker et al. [2011c] estimate ABJ's cost stickiness model using OLS regression with standard errors clustered by firm. Furthermore, Chen et al. [2011] include year dummies. Kama and Weiss [2010], on the other hand, estimate ABJ's cost stickiness model, using the regression technique of Fama and Macbeth [1973]. That is, they estimate the model separately for each year and then report mean across-year coefficient estimates and the associated t-statistics. When I emulate Chen et al. [2011] (Kama and Weiss [2010]) by using firm-clustered standard errors and including year dummies (by using Fama-Macbeth [1973] regression), my results again remain qualitatively unchanged (Panel F of Table 4.3).

4.5.7 Main Effect of Decrease Dummy

ABJ's cost stickiness model is simple and intuitive. However, it is problematic from an econometric point of view, because it does not include the main effect of the dummy variable that identifies sales decreases and is interacted with the change in sales. When I add the main effect of this decrease dummy variable to models [4.1] and [4.2], I obtain inferentially similar results (Panel G of Table 4.3).

4.5.8 Experienced Analysts

In my original analysis, I work with consensus forecasts constructed from individual forecasts made by both experienced and inexperienced analysts. This heterogeneity raises the question of whether my finding that analysts' early cost forecasts disregard cost stickiness is driven by forecasts made by inexperienced analysts. In order to answer this question, I restrict my sample to consensus forecasts constructed from individual forecasts made solely by analysts with at least three years of firm-specific forecasting experience, that is, by analysts who have issued at least one earnings forecast for the same firm in at least three prior years.[75] Focusing on

[75] When calculating the number of prior periods with earnings forecasts, I consider only forecasts that are made during the first 11 months of a particular fiscal year (see Clement [1999, 292]).

experienced analysts leads to similar results and identical conclusions (Panel H of Table 4.3).

4.6 Conclusion

The aim of this analysis is to contribute to an integration of management and financial accounting research topics, a research gap recently highlighted by Weiss [2010]. In order to do so, I combine cost stickiness with financial analysts' forecasts and analyze whether analysts' cost forecasts heed cost stickiness, that is, the observation that costs decrease less when sales fall than they increase when sales rise. Analysts rarely disclose their cost forecasts. Consequently, I calculate analysts' cost forecasts implicitly as the difference between forecasted sales and earnings.

As my main contribution, I find that analysts' cost forecasts disregard cost stickiness. In fact, analysts' cost forecasts are even anti-sticky, that is, costs are forecasted to decrease more when sales are predicted to fall than they are forecasted to increase when sales are predicted to rise. I attribute this disregard of cost stickiness in analysts' cost forecasts to a previously unexplored form of optimism in analysts' earnings forecasts. Analysts' earnings forecasts are not only "externally" optimistic, that is, too high with respect to actual earnings, but also "internally" optimistic, that is, too high with respect to forecasted sales. A further analysis of my results reveals that analysts overestimate cost decreases for falling sales to a greater extent than they underestimate cost increases for rising sales and that the disregard of cost stickiness in analysts' cost forecasts is restricted to early forecasts, that is, to forecasts issued well before the announcement date.

The finding that analysts overestimate cost decreases for falling sales to a greater extent than they underestimate cost increases for rising sales suggests that internal optimism is more than just a general byproduct of external optimism. Instead, analysts seem to specifically underestimate the reason for sticky cost behavior, that is, managers' hesitance to cut redundant resources. After all, analysts heavily rely on managerial information. Managers, in turn, probably do not want to inform analysts about their tendency to retain unutilized resources (e.g., to keep prestigious assets or longstanding employees), because they fear that analysts and investors will regard them as opportunistic or inefficient. Consequently, when sales are expected to fall and resources become idle, analysts are likely to erroneously expect managers to cut these resources and thus, they issue earnings forecasts that are too high with respect to the forecasted sales level. The finding that the disregard of cost stickiness in analysts' cost forecasts is restricted to early forecasts is consistent with the notion that, just like external optimism, internal optimism declines as the announcement date approaches.

My results are of interest to both analysts and investors. Analysts can benefit from my findings by becoming more aware of cost behavior and its underlying managerial incentives. They can increase the consistency, and potentially also the accuracy of their earnings and sales forecasts, if they ensure that these forecasts mirror the stickiness that characterizes actual cost behavior. Similarly, investors can take advantage of my results by critically checking analysts' earnings and sales forecasts for consistency with cost stickiness, before they use such forecasts as a basis for investment decisions.

5 Concluding Remarks

Understanding cost behavior is a fundamental element of cost accounting and the management of a firm. Deviating from the traditional assumption of symmetric cost behavior, numerous recent research studies show that costs are sticky, that is, they decrease less when sales fall than they increase when sales rise. Beginning with Anderson et al. [2003], accounting research explains this observation in terms of an alternative model in which costs arise due to deliberate adjustment decisions made by managers. When activity declines, forward-looking managers balance adjustment costs against those of temporarily keeping idle capacity, in order to maximize the long-term value of the firm. Additionally, self-interested managers are affected by different incentives, such as status considerations, which induce them to omit or delay reasonable resource reductions. A wide range of accounting research studies builds on this alternative model and addresses different characteristics and implications of sticky cost behavior. This doctoral thesis contributes to the field of research on cost stickiness in three distinct ways.

As the first contribution, I consider the development of research on sticky cost behavior in detail and provide a structured overview of the current research literature on cost stickiness. To the best of my knowledge, this chapter of my doctoral thesis is the first structured review which considers cost stickiness from all possible angles by incorporating each supporting and conflicting finding on the various different characteristics, causes, and implications of sticky cost behavior. The review in this doctoral thesis organizes the previous findings in terms of general, firm, industry and country-specific characteristics. Furthermore, I discuss all studies of managerial incentives influencing sticky cost behavior, as well as those criticizing the cost stickiness concept. Although the observation of asymmetric cost behavior provides important implications for both cost accounting methods and related financial areas, only a small number of research studies deals with the implications of cost stickiness for related areas. I present and analyze the few existing studies that combine cost stickiness with related research and point out the need for additional research that I then contribute through the research studies presented in Chapters 3 and 4.

As the second contribution, the study presented in Chapter 3 reveals important implications of cost stickiness for *fundamental analysis* by using the example of the information content of the SG&A ratio.[76] This key figure proves to be more complex than the common interpretation accommodates. According to the prevalent view, high or rising values of this ratio are regarded as inefficiency in cost management, exerting a *negative* impact on future profitability. By contrast, recent research literature presents potential explanations of a *positive* effect of a rising SG&A ratio on future performance, based mainly on cost stickiness (see Anderson et al. [2007]). According to the explanation based on the stickiness of costs, an increase in the SG&A ratio provides a positive signal in periods of falling demand, because it conveys positive managerial expectations. The rationale underlying this assumption is that managers do not reduce the SG&A ratio, since they assume the current decline in demand to be only temporary, which constitutes a positive signal for future firm performance.

My empirical analysis demonstrates that it is crucial to differentiate between whether an increase in the SG&A ratio occurs with *intent* to enhance profitability or merely results from insufficient cost control. As a proxy for managerial SG&A cost control, I use the past relationship of the individual SG&A ratio to its industry mean. Through this analysis, I find a positive impact of a rising SG&A ratio on future operating earnings for SG&A cost-efficient firms and a negative impact for SG&A cost-inefficient firms. This differentiation yields a stronger, more significant, and more persistent SG&A signal and provides incremental explanatory power beyond the differentiation by cost stickiness. However, the most meaningful SG&A signal can be created when both differentiation approaches, that is, cost stickiness and cost efficiency, are applied simultaneously. Further analyses reveal that the positive impact of SG&A investments is due to lower future cost of goods sold and that it is exceptionally strong if there is ample latitude for reducing these costs. This finding suggests that intended SG&A expenditures partially represent investments in operating efficiency. The results of the study are important to both managers and external users of financial statements.

As the third contribution, the research study presented in Chapter 4 yields important implications for the impact of cost stickiness on *financial analysts' forecasts*. In this study, I analyze whether analysts' cost forecasts consider the stickiness of costs. My empirical analysis shows that analysts' cost forecasts disregard

[76] The SG&A ratio measures the relation of selling, general, and administrative costs to sales.

cost stickiness.[77] These forecasts turn out to be even "anti-sticky", that is, costs are forecasted to decrease more when sales are predicted to fall than they are forecasted to increase when sales are predicted to rise. I attribute this disregard of cost stickiness in analysts' cost forecasts to a previously unexplored form of optimism in analysts' earnings forecasts. Analysts' earnings forecasts are not only "externally" optimistic, that is, too high with respect to actual earnings, but also "internally" optimistic, that is, too high with respect to forecasted sales. A further analysis suggests that analysts seem to particularly underestimate the reason for sticky cost behavior, that is, managers' hesitance to cut redundant resources. Previous research consistently documents that analysts heavily rely on managerial information. Managers, in turn, probably do not wish to inform analysts about their tendency to retain unutilized resources, because they fear that analysts and investors will regard them as opportunistic or inefficient. Consequently, when sales are expected to fall and resources become idle, analysts are likely to erroneously expect managers to cut these resources and thus, they issue earnings forecasts that are too high with respect to the forecasted sales level. These results are of interest to both analysts and investors.

Taken together, this doctoral thesis comprehensively reconciles the wide range of research on cost stickiness in a structured review and highlights the relevance of sticky cost behavior for related research fields by providing important implications for fundamental analysis and analysts' forecasts. The two empirical studies presented in this thesis offer a wide range of insights, but are inevitably subject to certain limitations. However, these limitations open up potential for future research. The analysis of cost stickiness and the information content of the SG&A ratio could, for instance, be further enhanced by analyzing the impact of changes in *individual* components of SG&A costs. Access to a large pool of itemized cost data at the firm level could overcome the limitation of the aggregated reporting of SG&A costs. Moreover, structured interviews with managers and additional proxies for managerial intent to invest in SG&A resources could potentially provide further insights into the effects of these investments. The analysis of cost stickiness and analysts' implied costs forecasts could be enhanced by introducing measures to differentiate more clearly between the effects of external and internal optimism. Additionally, structured

[77] Since financial analysts rarely disclose their cost forecasts, I calculate analysts' cost forecasts implicitly as the difference between forecasted sales and earnings.

interviews with analysts and a detailed evaluation of a variety of research reports could yield additional insights.

Apart from propositions for future research arising from the limitations and potential extensions of my empirical analyses, my structured review of the cost stickiness research literature also reveals several possibilities for future contributions to this research field. For instance, Balakrishnan and Gruca [2008] analyze variation in cost stickiness between different departments within hospitals. This approach of analyzing intra-firm variation in cost stickiness could be carried forward by conducting a similar analysis for firms in a competitive industry outside the health sector. Furthermore, Subramaniam and Weidenmier [2003] and Calleja et al. [2006] arrive at contradictory conclusions regarding the influence of the magnitude of activity changes on the stickiness of costs, while Balakrishnan et al. [2004] find no significant relationship. Future research could analyze this apparently complex relationship. Another potential direction for future research is to analyze the relative importance of the two main drivers of cost stickiness, adjustment costs and managerial incentives, in explaining the occurrence and extent of sticky cost behavior. Moreover, Banker et al. [2011c] respond to criticism of the prevailing approach of determining and explaining cost stickiness expressed by Anderson and Lanen [2009] and Balakrishnan et al. [2011]. No study so far has explicitly considered both sides of this controversy and thoroughly reconciled the conflicting arguments. Finally, and probably most importantly, as emphasized by Weiss [2010] and Banker et al. [2011c], the very limited number of research studies yielding implications of sticky cost behavior for related research areas constitutes a significant research gap. The empirical analyses presented in this doctoral thesis contribute substantially to filling this research gap. However, there remains considerable potential for future research to provide new insights into the consequences of sticky cost behavior.

References

Abarbanell, J. S., and V. L. Bernard. 1992. Tests of Analysts' Overreaction/ Underreaction to Earnings Information as an Explanation for Anomalous Stock Price Behavior. *The Journal of Finance* 47 (3): 1181–1207.

Abarbanell, J. S., and B. J. Bushee. 1997. Fundamental Analysis, Future Earnings, and Stock Prices. *Journal of Accounting Research* 35 (1): 1–24.

Anderson, M. C., R. D. Banker, L. Chen, and S. N. Janakiraman. 2004. Sticky Costs at Service Firms. Working paper, University of Texas at Dallas.

Anderson, M. C., R. D. Banker, R. Huang, and S. N. Janakiraman. 2007. Cost Behavior and Fundamental Analysis of SG&A Costs. *Journal of Accounting, Auditing and Finance* 22 (1): 1–28.

Anderson, M. C., R. D. Banker, and S. N. Janakiraman. 2003. Are Selling, General, and Administrative Costs "Sticky"? *Journal of Accounting Research* 41 (1): 47–63.

Anderson, S. W., C. X. Chen, and S. M. Young. 2005. Sticky Costs as Competitive Response: Evidence on Strategic Cost Management at Southwest Airlines. Working paper, Rice University and University of Southern California.

Anderson, S. W., and W. N. Lanen. 2009. Understanding Cost Management: What Can We Learn from the Empirical Evidence on "Sticky Costs?". Working paper, Rice University and University of Michigan.

Argilés, J. M., and J. García-Blandón. 2009. Cost Stickiness Revisited: Empirical Application for Farms. *Spanish Journal of Finance and Accounting* 38 (144): 579–605.

Atkinson, A. A., R. S. Kaplan, E. M. Matsumura, and S. M. Young. 2007. *Management Accounting. 5th edition.* Upper Saddle River, NJ: Prentice Hall.

Balakrishnan, R., and T. S. Gruca. 2008. Cost Stickiness and Core Competency: A Note. *Contemporary Accounting Research* 25 (4): 993–1006.

Balakrishnan, R., E. Labro, and N. S. Soderstrom. 2011. Cost Structure and Sticky Costs. Working paper, The University of Iowa, University of North Carolina, and University of Colorado.

Balakrishnan, R., M. J. Petersen, and N. S. Soderstrom. 2004. Does Capacity Utilization Affect the "Stickiness" of Cost? *Journal of Accounting, Auditing and Finance* 19 (3): 283–299.

Balakrishnan, R., and N. S. Soderstrom. 2008. Cross-Sectional Variation in Cost Stickiness. Working paper, The University of Ohio and University of Colorado.

Banker, R. D., D. Byzalov, and L. T. Chen. 2011a. Impact of Labor Laws on Cost Behavior. Working paper, Temple University and Peking University.

Banker, R. D., D. Byzalov, and J. M. Plehn-Dujowich. 2011b. Impact of Uncertainty on Cost Structure. Working paper, Temple University.

Banker, R. D., D. Byzalov, and J. M. Plehn-Dujowich. 2011c. Sticky Cost Behavior: Theory and Evidence. Working paper, Temple University.

Banker, R. D., and L. Chen. 2006a. Labor Market Characteristics and Cross-Country Differences in Cost Stickiness. Working paper, Temple University and Georgia State University.

Banker, R. D., and L. Chen. 2006b. Predicting Earnings Using a Model Based on Cost Variability and Cost Stickiness. *The Accounting Review* 81 (2): 285–307.

Banker, R. D., M. Ciftci, and R. Mashruwala. 2006a. The Effect of Prior-Period Sales Changes on Cost Behavior. Working paper, Temple University, The University of Texas at Dallas, and Washington University in St. Louis.

Banker, R. D., M. Ciftci, and R. Mashruwala. 2011d. Managerial Optimism and Cost Behavior, Temple University, SUNY at Binghamton, and University of Illinois at Chicago.

Banker, R. D., R. Huang, and R. Natarajan. 2006b. Does SG&A Expenditure Create a Long-Lived Asset? Working paper, Temple University, Baruch College-City University of New York, and The University of Texas at Dallas.

Banker, R. D., R. Huang, and R. Natarajan. 2011e. Equity Incentives and Long-Term Value Created by SG&A Expenditure. *Contemporary Accounting Research* 28 (3): 794–830.

Banker, R. D., and H. H. Johnston. 1993. An Empirical Study of Cost Drivers in the U.S. Airline Industry. *The Accounting Review* 68 (3): 576–601.

Basu, S. 1997. The Conservatism Principle and the Asymmetric Timeliness of Earnings. *Journal of Accounting and Economics* 24 (1): 3–37.

Baumgarten, D., Berens, M., and C. Homburg. 2011. Analysts‘ Implied Cost Forecasts and Cost Stickiness. Working paper, University of Cologne.

Baumgarten, D., Bonenkamp, U., and C. Homburg. 2010. The Information Content of the SG&A Ratio. *Journal of Management Accounting Research* 22 (1): 1–24.

Bernstein, L., and J. Wild. 1998. *Financial statement analysis. 6th edition.* New York: McGraw-Hill.

Beyer, R. 1963. *Profitability Accounting for Planning and Control.* New York: Ronald Press Company.

Bowen, R. M., A. K. Davis, and D. A. Matsumoto. 2002. Do Conference Calls Affect Analysts' Forecasts? *The Accounting Review* 77 (2): 285–316.

Calleja, K., M. Steliaros, and D. C. Thomas. 2006. A Note on Cost Stickiness: Some International Comparisons. *Management Accounting Research* 17 (2): 127–140.

Cannon, J. N. 2011. Determinants of "Sticky Costs:" An Analysis of Cost Behavior using United States Air Transportation Industry Data. Working paper, Iowa State University.

Caylor, M. L., and T. J. Lopez. 2010. Cost Behavior and Executive Compensation. Working paper, University of South Carolina and University of Alabama.

Chen, E. H., and W. J. Dixon. 1972. Estimates of Parameters of a Censored Regression Sample. *Journal of the American Statistical Association* 67 (339): 664–671.

Chen, C. X., H. Lu, and T. Sougiannis. 2011. The Agency Problem, Corporate Governance, and the Asymmetrical Behavior of Selling, General, and Administrative Costs. *Contemporary Accounting Research* (forthcoming).

Clement, M. B. 1999. Analyst Forecast Accuracy: Do Ability, Resources, and Portfolio Complexity Matter? *Journal of Accounting and Economics* 27 (3): 285–303.

Das, S., C. B. Levine, and K. Sivaramakrishnan. 1998. Earnings Predictability and Bias in Analysts' Earnings Forecasts. *The Accounting Review* 73 (2): 277–294.

De Medeiros, O. R., and P. de Souza Costa. 2004. Cost Stickiness in Brazilian Firms. Working paper, Universidade de Brasilia.

Dieckman, E., and T. White. 2005. Seizing Control of SG&A. *Financial Executive* 21 (2): 20–23.

Dierynck, B., and A. Renders. 2009. Earnings Management Incentives and the Asymmetric Behavior of Labor Costs. Working paper, Katholieke Universiteit Leuven.

Dugar, A., and S. Nathan. 1995. The Effect of Investment Banking Relationships on Financial Analysts' Earnings Forecasts and Investment Recommendations. *Contemporary Accounting Research* 12 (1): 131–160.

Elgers, P. T., and M. H. Lo. 1994. Reductions in Analysts' Annual Earnings Forecast Errors Using Information in Prior Earnings and Security Returns. *Journal of Accounting Research* 32 (2): 290–303.

Ely, K. M. 1991. Interindustry Differences in the Relation between Compensation and Firm Performance Variables. *Journal of Accounting Research* 29 (1): 37–58.

Ertimur, Y., W. J. Mayew, and S. R. Stubben. 2011. Analyst Reputation and the Issuance of Disaggregated Earnings Forecasts to I/B/E/S. *Review of Accounting Studies* 16 (1): 29–58.

Fairfield, P. M., R. J. Sweeney, and T. L. Yohn. 1996. Accounting Classification and the Predictive Content of Earnings. *The Accounting Review* 71 (3): 337–355.

Fama, E. F., and K. R. French. 1997. Industry Costs of Equity. *Journal of Financial Economics* 43 (2): 153–193.

Fama, E. F., and J. D. MacBeth. 1973. Risk, Return and Equilibrium: Empirical Tests. *Journal of Political Economy* 81 (3): 607–636.

Francis, J., and D. Philbrick. 1993. Analysts' Decisions as Products of a Multi-Task Environment. *Journal of Accounting Research* 31 (2): 216–230.

Garrison, R., E. Noreen, and P. Brewer. 2009. *Managerial Accounting. 13th edition.* New York: McGraw-Hill.

Givoly, D., C. Hayn, and R. Lehavy. 2009. The Quality of Analysts' Cash Flow Forecasts. *The Accounting Review* 84 (6): 1877–1911.

Goux, D., E. Maurin, and M. Pauchet. 2001. Fixed-Term Contracts and the Dynamics of Labour Demand. *European Economic Review* 45 (3): 533–552.

Gow, I. D., G. Ormazabal, and D. J. Taylor. 2010. Correcting for Cross-Sectional and Time-Series Dependence in Accounting Research. *The Accounting Review* 85 (2): 483–512.

Gu, Z., and J. S. Wu. 2003. Earnings Skewness and Analyst Forecast Bias. *Journal of Accounting and Economics* 35 (1): 5–29.

Hay, D., C. de Villiers, and Z. J. Zhang. 2011. Audit Fee Stickiness. Working paper, The University of Auckland Business School.

He, D. S., T. Shimizu, and J. Teruya. 2010. Sticky Selling, General, and Administrative Cost Behavior and its Changes in Japan. *Global Journal of Business Research* 4 (4): 1–10.

Homburg, C., and J. Nasev. 2008. How Timely are Earnings when Costs are Sticky? Implications for the Link between Conditional Conservatism and Cost Stickiness. Working paper, University of Cologne.

Jensen, M. C., and W. H. Meckling. 1976. Theory of the Firm: Managerial Behavior, Agency Costs and Ownership Structure. *Journal of Financial Economics* 3 (4): 305–360.

Kajiwara, T., and K. Yasukata. 2011. Are "Sticky Costs" the Result of Deliberate Decision of Managers? Working paper, Kinki University and Kobe University.

Kama, I., and D. Weiss. 2010. Do Managers' Deliberate Decisions Induce Sticky Costs? Working paper, Tel Aviv University.

Karatzias, K. 2009. *Cost Stickiness and the Implications for Future Performance: Evaluating the Moderating Effect of the Investment Opportunity Set on the Relationship between Cost Stickiness and Future Performance.* Saarbrücken: Lambert Academic Publishing.

Keung, E. C. 2010. Do Supplementary Sales Forecasts Increase the Credibility of Financial Analysts' Earnings Forecasts? *The Accounting Review* 85 (6): 2047–2074.

Kim, M., and J. Prather-Kinsey. 2010. An Additional Source of Financial Analysts' Earnings Forecast Errors: Imperfect Adjustments for Cost Behavior. *Journal of Accounting, Auditing* and *Finance* 25 (1): 27–51.

Kothari, S. P. 2001. Capital Markets Research in Accounting. *Journal of Accounting and Economics* 31 (1-3): 105–231.

Lang, M. H., and R. J. Lundholm. 1996. Corporate Disclosure Policy and Analyst Behavior. *The Accounting Review* 71 (4): 467–492.

Lazere, C. 1996. Holding the Line on SG&A. *CFO: The Magazine for Senior Financial Executives* 12 (12): 28–36.

Lev, B., and S. R. Thiagarajan. 1993. Fundamental Information Analysis. *Journal of Accounting Research* 31 (2): 190–215.

Libby, R., J. E. Hunton, H.-T. Tan, and N. Seybert. 2008. Relationship Incentives and the Optimistic/ Pessimistic Pattern in Analysts' Forecasts. *Journal of Accounting Research* 46 (1): 173–198.

Lim, T. 2001. Rationality and Analysts' Forecast Bias. *The Journal of Finance* 56 (1): 369–385.

Mak, Y. T., and M. L. Roush. 1994. Flexible Budgeting and Variance Analysis in an Activity-Based Costing Environment. *Accounting Horizons* 8 (2): 93–103.

Malcom, R. E. 1991. Overhead Control Implications of Activity Costing. *Accounting Horizons* 5 (4): 69–78.

McNichols, M., and P. C. O'Brien. 1997. Self-Selection and Analyst Coverage. *Journal of Accounting Research* 35 (3): 167–199.

Mest, D. P., and E. Plummer. 2003. Analysts' Rationality and Forecast Bias: Evidence from Sales Forecasts. *Review of Quantitative Finance and Accounting* 21 (2): 103–122.

Noreen, E. 1991. Conditions under Which Activity-Based Cost Systems Provide Relevant Costs. *Journal of Management Accounting Research* 3: 159–168.

Noreen, E., and N. Soderstrom. 1994. Are Overhead Costs Strictly Proportional to Activity? *Journal of Accounting and Economics* 17 (1–2): 255–278.

Noreen, E., and N. Soderstrom. 1997. The Accuracy of Proportional Cost Models: Evidence from Hospital Service Departments. *Review of Accounting Studies* 2 (1): 89–114.

Özkaya, H., and S. Yükcü. 2011. Cost Behavior in Turkish Firms: Are Selling, General and Administrative Costs and Total Operating Costs "Sticky"? *World of Accounting Science* 13 (3): 1–27.

Ou, J. A. 1990. The Information Content of Nonearnings Accounting Numbers as Earnings Predictors. *Journal of Accounting Research* 28 (1): 144–163.

Petersen, M. A. 2009. Estimating Standard Errors in Finance Panel Data Sets: Comparing Approaches. *The Review of Financial Studies* 22 (1): 435–480.

Porporato, M., and E. Werbin. 2010. Active Cost Management in Banks: Evidence of Sticky Costs in Argentina, Brazil and Canada. Working paper, SAS-York University and National University of Cordoba.

Ramnath, S., S. Rock, and P. Shane. 2008. The Financial Analyst Forecasting Literature: A Taxonomy with Suggestions for Further Research. *International Journal of Forecasting* 24 (1): 34–75.

Richardson, S., S. H. Teoh, and P. D. Wysocki. 1999. Tracking Analysts' Forecasts over the Annual Earnings Horizon: Are Analysts' Forecasts Optimistic or Pessimistic? Working paper, University of Michigan Business School.

Richardson, S., S. H. Teoh, and P. D. Wysocki. 2004. The Walk-Down to Beatable Analyst Forecasts: The Role of Equity Issuance and Insider Trading Incentives. *Contemporary Accounting Research* 21 (4): 885–924.

Sloan, R. G. 1996. Do Stock Prices Fully Reflect Information in Accruals and Cash Flows About Future Earnings? *The Accounting Review* 71 (3): 289–315.

Sloan, R. G. 2001. Discussion of: "Contextual Fundamental Analysis through the Prediction of Extreme Returns". *Review of Accounting Studies* 6 (2-3): 191–195.

Spence, M. 1984. Cost Reduction, Competition, and Industry Performance. *Econometrica* 52 (1): 101–121.

Stickney, C. P., and P. R. Brown. 1999. *Financial Reporting and Financial Statement Analysis: A Strategic Perspective. 4th edition.* Orlando: Dryden.

Strube, E. 1936. Kostenremanenz und Beschäftigungsschwankungen. *Zeitschrift für Handelswissenschaftliche Forschung* 30 (10): 505-541.

Subramaniam C., and M. L. Weidenmier. 2003. Additional Evidence on the Sticky Behavior of Costs. Working paper, Texas Christian University.

Weiss, D. 2010. Cost Behavior and Analysts' Earnings Forecasts. *The Accounting Review* 85 (4): 1441–1471.

West, D. A. 2003. Three Financial Strategies. *Journal of Health Care Finance* 30 (1): 10–22.

Wiersma, E. 2010. The Impact of the Reward Structure on Stickiness. Working paper, VU University Amsterdam.

White, H. 1980. A Heteroskedasticity-Consistent Covariance Matrix Estimator and a Direct Test for Heteroskedasticity. *Econometrica* 48 (4): 817–838.

www.ingramcontent.com/pod-product-compliance
Lightning Source LLC
Chambersburg PA
CBHW071351230926
51846CB00002B/512
* 9 7 8 3 8 3 4 9 4 1 3 0 5 *